The Story of India for Children

The Story of
India
for Children

Gratian Vas

Illustrated by
Mrinal Mitra

BLOSSOM BOOKS

Blossom Books (P) Ltd.
15 Gulmohar Commercial Complex
Sector 15, Noida 201 301, U.P. India

Published by Blossom Books (P) Ltd. 1997

ISBN 81-87159-00-6

First Printed 1997

Revised Edition 1998

Revised Edition 1999

Reprinted 2000

Printed At Icon Press New Delhi

To
My daughters
Piya (14) & Kirin (9)
who inspired this book.

CONTENTS

Introduction

As with my other books, preparing this one has been an opportunity for me to go back in thought to my childhood. As a child one never got to read the history of India in one book. In school it was taught in bits and pieces called 'eras' and 'ages' which read more like a chronology of dates and events and failed to hold the attention of young minds. There were no illustrated books which we could read, understand and enjoy.

Later when I got to study Indian history seriously and in greater detail, I did not fail to notice that it had all the ingredients of an exciting story if presented in language and form appropriate for young readers. In a panorama of events spreading from prehistoric times to the present day, it had the bold adventures of Rama, Arjuna and Shivaji, spiritual pursuits of Mahavira, Buddha, Sankara and Guru Nanak; political intrigues of Chandragupta Maurya and Chanakya; amusing behaviour of temperamental rulers; charming romances of princes and princesses, rise and fall of empires and of course the great saga of India's freedom struggle. What a wonderful story book would that be to put in the hands of children! This remained my dream.

Thirty years later, the scene hadn't changed much – there still isn't an illustrated history book for children in colour. As I saw my own children growing up, I decided that the time was appropriate to put on paper the dazzling pictures of Indian history which had filled my mind for so long! And this book is the outcome.

Five thousand years is a long stretch of time and India is a vast country. Many events were taking place in different parts at any given time. Therefore, not everything in India's history could possibly have been squeezed into a book like this. I have focussed on very important and exciting events to give the child a bird's eye-view of India's history. However, these various episodes fit together, like pieces in a jig-saw to make one big picture. I've strived to make this picture plain yet beautiful.

Many people helped make this book what it is through their invaluable contributions and I find it difficult to adequately express my gratitude and appreciation.

C.N. Penn-Anthony, a distinguished and much respected former member of the Indian Administrative Service who went through the manuscript meticulously, made corrections, suggested improvement, and made incisive comments leading me to think afresh on many points. Besides generously sharing his knowledge on the subject, for the most part he contributed to the chapters on post independence period.

Nripendra Misra, I.A.S. for his keen interest, steady encouragement and enthusiastic support from start to finish.

Asharani, editor and producer of many a book, for her critical observations and informed guidance.

Suchitra Vedant for doing an excellent job of final editing .

Loreta, my wife; **Piya** and **Kirin** my daughters, who had often to fend for themselves on important occasions, for being patient and assisting me quietly in their own ways.

Mrinal Mitra for adding mystery and magic to this great story with his lavish illustrations.

Jagdish Joshi, another artist of international repute for his pictures — *Settled Life* (p.12), *Pyjama and Kaftan, Salwar Khameez* (p.80), *Dadabhai Naoroji* and *Surendranath Banerjee* (p.144) *Azad* and *Bhagat Singh* (p.154).

Dona Mukherjee for the chart on *Mughal Dynasty* (p.100), *The Mughal Coins* (p.101), *Indian Soldiers Atop Captured Tank* (p.182), *The Satellite Launch* (p.191), *Computers, Satellite and Power Project* (p.192).

Apple Publishing Technology Centre, New Delhi for All the Maps.

I wish to acknowledge here the many existing works which I have used as references: *A Children's History of India*, Sheila Dhar; *Discovery of India*, Pandit Jawaharlal Nehru; *History and Culture of Indian People*, Bharatiya Vidya Mandir; *An Illustrated History of India*, Tulsi Vatsal; *The Wonder that was India* (Part-I), A.L. Basham; *The Wonder that was India* (Part II), S.A.A. Rizvi; *A History of India* (Vol I), Romila Thapar; *A History of India* (Vol II), Percival Spear; *An Advanced History of India*, R.C. Majumdar, H.C. Raychaudhuri and Kalikinkar Datta; *Modern History of India*, Romila Thapar; *Making of Modern India*, Mac Nicol; *History of Freedom Movement in India*, R.C. Majumdar; *Freedom Struggle*, Bipin Chandra, Amales Tripathi and Barun De; *From Akbar to Aurangzeb*, W.H. Moreland; *History of the Sikhs*, Cunningham; *History of Mahrattas*, Grant Duff; *Introduction to the Study of Indian History*, D.D. Kosambi; *A History of South India*, K. A. Nilakanta Sastri; *Early History of India*, Vincent A Smith; *The Indus Civilization*, R.E.M. Wheeler; *The Roots of Ancient India*, Walter A. Fairservis Jr. *Indian Struggle for Freedom*, Satyavrata Ghosh.

Gratian Vas

Gratian Vas worked as teacher, headmaster and principal for seven years in Lucknow and then moved full-time to the pursuit of writing for children. In the past 25 years he has written over 900 educational and general books for young readers. He lives in New Delhi.

Mrinal Mitra, a graduate from the College of Art, Calcutta is a renouned illustrator of children's books. Among his many awards and honours is the prestigious 'Noma Concours' for Picture Book Illustrators organised by the Asian Cultural Centre for UNESCO. He lives in Toronto, Canada.

Pots and Pans Tell A Story

Settled Life

History is about things that happened in the past. First of all it is about the lives of great men. Some were great rulers. They fought battles and conquered lands. Sometimes they made people happy and sometimes unhappy. Some of the great men were famous teachers, writers, explorers, scientists, artists and musicians. They performed great deeds and showed people how to lead good lives.

Besides great men and their lives history is also about ordinary people. It tells us about how they lived, how they got their food, how they built their villages and cities, the clothes they wore and the food they ate.

History is like an interesting and exciting series of stories. However, these stories are not like the many fairy tales you have read. They are not about fairies, princes and enchanted lands. These are stories about real people and the things that really happened.

Most of these stories are recent and have come to us from books. Many thousands of years ago people did not have paper nor did they know the art of printing. They wrote on stone, palm leaves, metal plates, the barks of trees and on animal skins. Still earlier people did not know how to write. How then do we know about those times? In recent years people have dug below the ground and discovered old cities buried beneath. We can learn a lot about the people who lived in the cities by looking carefully at the things found there. The sharp stones they hunted with, the pots and pans they used, the beads and bangles and necklaces they wore, have been found in some places and tell us about the life of the people who used them.

For example, stone implements found in several parts of India show that early man lived here about 17,00,000 years ago. He knew how to make sharp-edged tools by hitting stone against stone. He chose rock which broke conveniently but was strong enough to cut, grind, split and scrape. His tool-kit included the chopper, discoid, flake, scraper and even a crude variety of handaxe! We call him **Paleolithic**, or *Old Stone Age* man. By about 10,000 B.C. people who had thus far been hunters and gatherers had learned how to tame wild animals and grow crops. Gradually they began to live settled life in small villages with mud brick huts. We call these the **Neolithic** or *New Stone Age* people.

History tells us about the past. Therefore, dates of events are quite important. They give us an idea of when they happened. When you read history books you'll often find the letters B.C. and A.D. after or before dates. B.C. stands for Before Christ; A.D. stands for Anno Domini which in Latin means in the year of our Lord. Historical dates are counted from the year of the birth of Christ.

Tool-kit

Early Man

13

Surprises in the Mound!

A Toy

A Seal

People have been living in India for several thousand years. But we had no way of knowing how they really lived.

About a hundred and fifty years ago, some men were building a railway line between Karachi and Lahore. While digging the earth they came across some bricks lying near a mound. The bricks were so good that they used them to lay the railway tracks! Even before this, for many years, people of the place had been using these bricks to build their homes! They did not know that these bricks were about 3,000 years old!

The villagers who lived there, had, for years called this place **Mohenjo-Daro,** which in Sindhi means 'the mound of the dead.' Later, people began to dig up the area. Buried beneath the mound were a number of big surprises! These led to the discovery of the two great ancient cities, **Harappa** and **Mohenjo-Daro.**

Over 1,000 such sites have so far been located and more are being found every year. Some of these sites are large enough to be called cities: **Harappa, Mohenjo-Daro, Chanhu-Daro** (Sindh), **Dholavira** and **Lothal** (Gujarat), **Kalibangan** (Rajasthan), **Banwali** (Haryana). The sites discovered so far are spread over a vast area: from the river **Oxus** in Afghanistan to river **Narmada** in the south, from the **Makran** coast in the west to **Meerut** in the north. It is an area, more than a million square kilometres in size!

Everyday Life

This discovery was hailed as a great event all over the world. Until then it was believed that India did not have a past of any great significance and that it was only in places such as **Egypt** and **Mesopotamia** that great civilizations had flourished. In India, civilization was supposed to have existed only for the past 3,000 years. Now at one stroke the findings in the Indus Valley pushed back India's history by nearly 2,000 years! From what was found here, we have come to know a lot about how people lived 5,000 years ago.

Cities were built to a plan. Houses were built of burnt bricks, with square courtyards, bathrooms and drains to carry the dirty water away. The streets were broad and straight so that chariots and bullock carts could move easily.

The most important building that has been found at Mohenjo-Daro is a great bath-house. It had a watertight tank 39 feet long, 23 feet wide and 8 feet deep. It was set in a courtyard surrounded by verandahs and a

15

number of rooms. It had flights of steps at two ends leading to the floor. There was a well to supply fresh water and drainage to empty the tank.

To the west of the great bath-house was a large granary. The grain stored there was not only used by local people but also exchanged for other things from different countries.

From the many statues found among the ruins we come to know a lot about the way people lived. The men wore robes which left one shoulder bare. The women kept long hair. They wore necklaces of beads and ornaments of ivory. The children had beautiful toys including toy animals which could nod their heads.

Among the people were skilled craftsmen who could make fine pots of clay and simple implements from copper and bronze. They even made fine cloth out of cotton. They knew how to write and draw. Scholars are now even able to decipher the script used by these people.

The seals found there tell us about the animals they reared and the gods and goddesses they worshipped. There was a **Divine Mother** and a god who was very much like **Shiva.** Most people were farmers. We do not know if they had a king, though a stone figure discovered here in 1927 is said to be that of a priest-king.

It is interesting to note that weapons were not found. Their cities were not carefully fortified. This means that these people were not fighters. They lived in peace and did not wish to conquer other lands. In this respect they were far advanced than we are!

The area is now a dry and barren land. But long ago it was green and fertile and, perhaps, thick forests grew there. The drawings on the seals show animals such as the water-buffalo, the tiger, the rhinoceros and the elephant. These animals could have lived only in big forests.

All along it was thought that Mohenjo-Daro, Harappa and some other cities discovered later, were built only along the river Indus. New research has shown that nearly two thirds of the sites were along another river, **Saraswati** which is now

The Great Bath-house

xtinct. Accordingly archeologists ave renamed the civilization as

ndus-Saraswati Civilization.

India gets her name from Indus, *'ndoi* in Greek means the people rho lived near the river Indus) also alled Sindhu. The land through rhich the river flows was once a part f India and, as you'll read later, it as much to do with the story of our ountry. Some years ago this land ras separated from India and became art of a new country called

akistan.

What really happened to the great idus Valley people? No one really nows. Some think that violent tribes >ming from elsewhere conquered em. Others are of the opinion that e Great Indian Desert crept slowly in and forced the people to move elsewhere. Soon they were forgotten. Years went by and their great cities lay buried under sand!

Planned cities, brick houses, clay pots, use of metals, woven cloth, toys and ornaments, may mean nothing much to us today. But just think of the world 5,000 years ago. From what has been discovered we know that in most parts of the world people living during that period were still wild and lived in caves, wearing animal skins, using stones for weapons and eating raw meat!

It is said that these intelligent people, from the days before history was written, were forgotten and thousands of years went by. Now, slowly, their story is being dug out from beneath the ground.

Indus-Saraswati Civilization - Sites

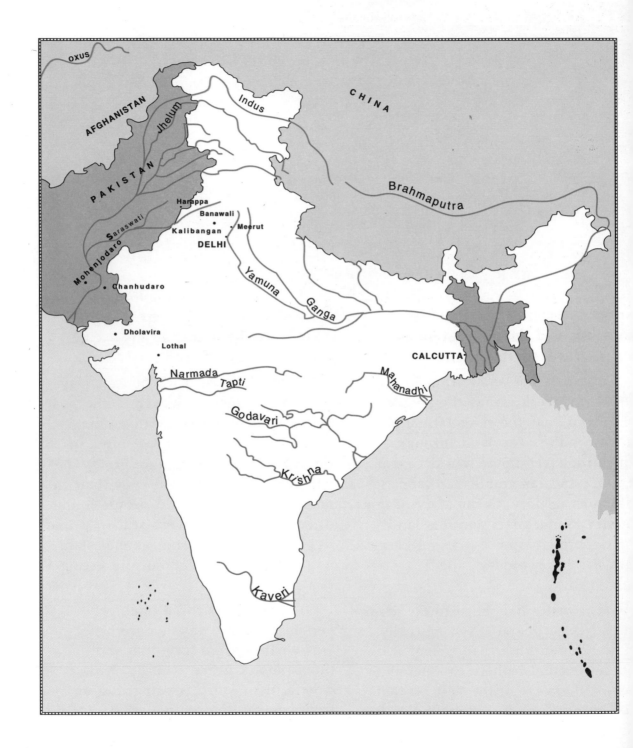

Indus-Saraswati Civilization - Area

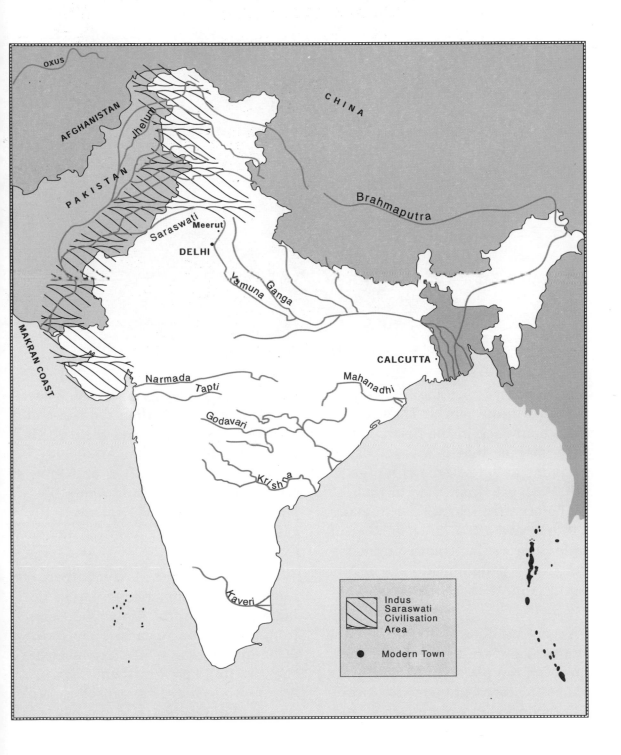

Visitors from Across the Mountains

The Aryans

The Himalayas are the highest mountains in the world. They form India's boundary in the north. One would imagine that it was impossible for anyone to enter India from the north. And yet, from time to time, even before man learnt how to make ships and aircraft, a large number of people came to this country from the north. These people made use of little gaps in mountains called passes, to cross them.

Among the first to arrive were the **Aryans**. They are believed to have come from the plains of Central Asia perhaps in search of better pastures for their flocks and more fertile land to grow crops. They came as settlers and not as a destroying army. They brought with them their women and children, their cattle and their goods. They also did not come all at once. They came as if in waves and first settled down in the land along the river Indus. Later they spread eastwards along the Yamuna and the Ganga.

When the Aryans arrived, there were already other people living in India. Their way of life was different from that of the Aryans. They spoke a different language. So there must have been friction between them. The Aryans rode horses and used swords as weapons so they won the battles and pushed the original inhabitants out of their land. But as time went by, the Aryans and the displaced people became friends and began to live together in peace. The Aryans, who had been cowherds, moving from one place to another, now settled down in villages and took to farming.

We are able to learn a lot about the Aryans from the books they have left us. These books are called the **Vedas** and are, perhaps, the oldest books in the world. They are four in number — the **Rigveda,** the **Yajurveda,** the **Samaveda** and the **Atharvaveda**. These books contain hymns which the people sang to their gods, and therefore, do not tell us much about kings and their conquests. But by studying them carefully we have come to know a great deal about the people's lives and customs.

The meaning of the Vedas is explained in detail in the books called the **Upanishads.** In the beginning the Vedas and the Upanishads were not written down. The students had to learn all the hymns by heart. And, as the hymns were considered sacred, not a single word could be left out!

The Vedas were written during a later period in **Sanskrit**. This is one of the greatest gifts the Aryans have left us. Sanskrit is a language which developed after the Aryans came to India. Most of India's ancient books are written in Sanskrit. Many of the languages we speak today, such as Hindi, Bengali and Marathi have evolved from Sanskrit.

The Leader

21

Among the early Aryans, the oldest member of the tribe was regarded as the leader. Later the most capable warrior was chosen as the chief. Soon he began to take on more powers and the people had to accept him as the king. This king, however, did not live in a palace nor did he collect taxes. His powers were kept in check by two assemblies called the *Sabha* and the *Samiti*. These assemblies consisted of elders, both men and women.

The Aryans were chiefly shepherds. They considered the cow very precious. The value of all other things was measured in terms of number of cows. Soon they settled down as farmers; forests were burnt or cut down to clear the land to sow crops. Initially the land belonged to everyone in the village but later it was divided among families. The villages had carpenters who made chariots, carts and ploughs. The metal workers made weapons and utensils. They could even make horse-shoes and iron-ends for ploughs. The weavers spun cloth of wool and cotton. They bought and sold things within their community and also with others.

The Aryans worshipped nature. They supposed that the sun and wind and the other forces of nature were gods who lived in heaven and rode across the sky in golden chariots. They had 33 chief gods. The people believed that these gods could be kept happy with devotion and gifts! Their chief god was **Indra,** the powerful god of storm and of war. **Agni** the fire god and **Varuna** the sky god were the other important gods.

When the Aryans first came to India they were divided into three groups — the warriors, the priests and the cultivators. These were not fixed classes or castes. Membership to these groups was determined by the occupation one followed and not by birth. People could choose what they wanted to do in life. Gradually the rules of castes became more and more strict. The warriors and priests began to look upon themselves as better human beings than the cultivators and labourers. And the three main groups, the **Brahmins,** the **Kshatriyas,** the **Vaishyas** began to think there were some people whom they should totally avoid. Such people were called untouchables! This was something really sad and shameful. It made the people falsely believe that some human beings were better than the others. In the years that followed it

Teaching

others. In the years that followed it made the Indian people weak by dividing them into groups among themselves.

In the course of time, the Aryans spread throughout north India and established powerful kingdoms. The south of India had its own people. They had their own kingdoms and cities and people with different languages and customs. For a long time the Aryans and the people of the south, who were called **Dravidians,** remained quite apart from each other. By and by the Aryans, especially their sages, began to visit the south. From them the people of the south learnt Sanskrit, some of their customs and above all about the Vedas. The Aryans learnt many things from the people of the south. Hundreds of years passed and the people of the north and south mingled with each other and began to live in the same

way. There was no south or north now, but one big country — Bharatavarsha or India.

The Early Aryan Settlement

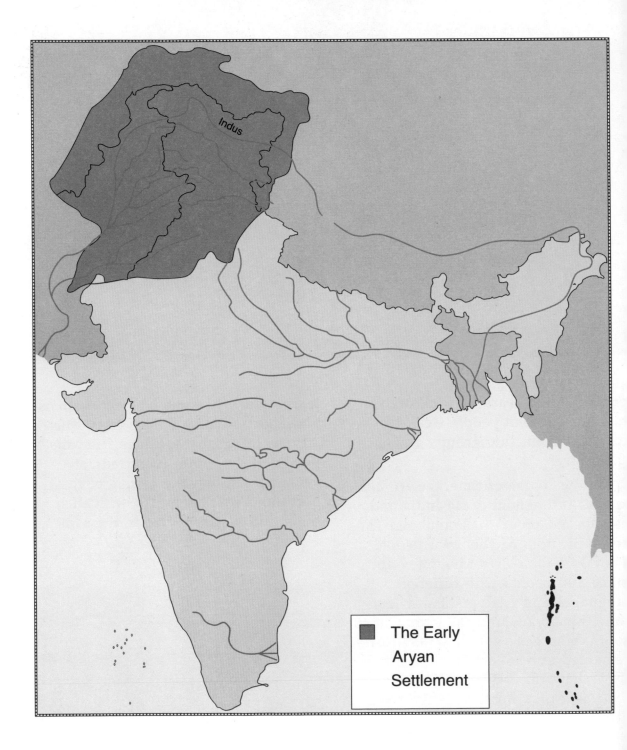

Indus

The Early
Aryan
Settlement

The Early Kingdoms

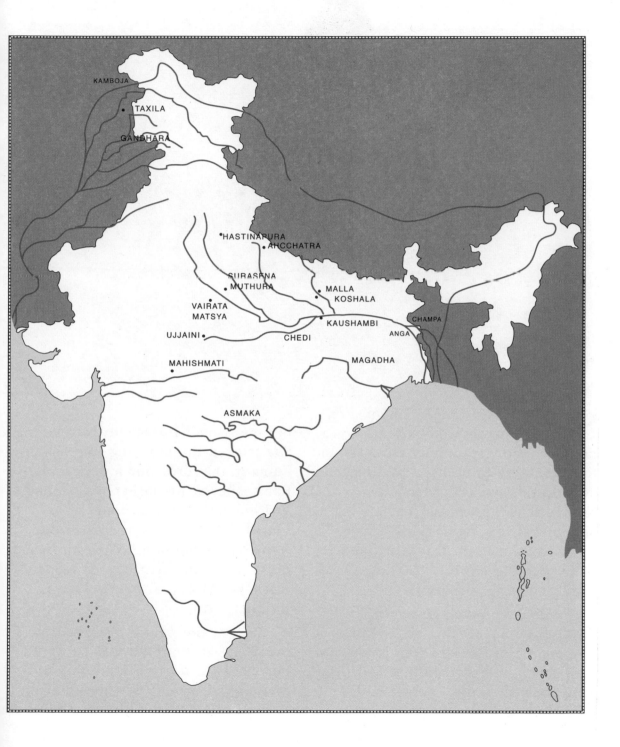

KAMBOJA

TAXILA

GANDHARA

HASTINAPURA

AHCCHATRA

SURASENA
MUTHURA

MALLA
KOSHALA

VAIRATA
MATSYA

KAUSHAMBI

CHAMPA

UJJAINI

CHEDI

ANGA

MAHISHMATI

MAGADHA

ASMAKA

Rama and Sita

Life in the Forest

Stories of heroes and heroines were popular among people of all ages, and they continue to be liked by everyone even to this day. Some scholars believe that the story of Rama's adventures, his fights with demons in the forest and with **Ravana,** the King of Lanka, is a story of the Aryans slowly moving into south India.

Rama was the eldest son of **Dasharatha**, the king of Ayodhya. The people of the kingdom loved him very much and wanted him to be the king after his father. But he had a step-mother, **Kaikeyi,** who wanted her own son **Bharata** to become king. She tricked the old king into sending Rama to the forest for fourteen years. Rama obeyed his father's command and left the palace to live in the **Dandaka** forest at the foot of the **Vindhya** mountains. With him went his young wife **Sita,** the daughter of **Raja Janaka**, and his brother **Lakshmana.**

Back at the palace everybody was sad. King Dasharatha was so upset that he died of grief. Bharata who loved his brother Rama very much, refused to sit on the throne. The whole

26

kingdom was plunged into a gloom.

In the forest, life for Rama, Sita and Lakshmana was very hard. They had none of the comforts they enjoyed at the palace. They faced danger and hardship at every step. Rama and Lakshmana had to fight many *rakshasas* or demons who tried to harm them.

One day, **Surpanaka**, the sister of the demon-king Ravana saw Lakshmana. She liked him so much that she wanted to marry him. Lakshmana did not want to marry her. But Surpanaka wouldn't let him go. Lakshmana was so angry that he cut her nose off with his sword.

Surpanaka ran to her brother and told him what Lakshmana had done to her. Ravana was furious with rage and vowed to take revenge. He made a wicked plan to teach Lakshmana a lesson. He called **Mareecha,** his uncle and sent him to Rama's hut disguised as a deer.

Sita was so charmed by the deer that she wanted it for her own. Rama promised to capture it for her and went after the deer. Lakshmana was ordered to stay back at the hut with Sita. After a while they heard Rama call to Lakshmana for help. Lakshmana was puzzled. Still he did not want to leave Sita alone in the forest. But on Sita's insistence he went out to help Rama. But Rama had not called out for help at all. It was the cunning Mareecha who had imitated

Rama's voice. Lakshmana had been tricked.

All along Ravana had been hiding behind the bushes. As soon as Lakshmana left, he caught hold of Sita and carried her off to his kingdom.

Rama Fights Ravana

27

Rama is Crowned King

the island of Lanka. Rama could not capture the deer, for there was no deer at all! When he returned to the hut empty-handed, he found Sita gone. He knew at once that a cruel trick had been played upon him. He was stricken with grief but vowed to search for Sita and bring her back. Lakshmana was even more upset that he had failed to protect his brother's wife. He went with his brother in search of Sita.

After many days of search and untold hardships, the two brothers met **Sugriva,** the king of the monkeys. Sugriva and his minister **Hanuman** promised to help them find Sita. It was soon discovered that Sita was being held prisoner by Ravana on the island of Lanka. The army of monkeys brought large stones and built a bridge across the sea for Rama to cross over to the island. Once on the island, Rama fought the fearful ten-headed demon king Ravana and killed him. Rama and Sita were together again.

The fourteen years of Rama's stay in the forest too had come to an end. He could now return to Ayodhya. When the people of Ayodhya heard of Rama's return, their joy knew no bounds. There were celebrations everywhere. When Rama was away, Bharata had ruled the kingdom in his name. Now Rama was crowned king. He ruled for many years. People were very happy with his just and peaceful rule.

The wonderful story of Rama and Sita is called the **Ramayana.** It was written by a sage called **Valmiki.**

The Pandavas and the Kauravas

One of the most famous kingdoms of ancient India was that of the **Kurus.** They had occupied the area near Delhi and had their capital at **Hastinapur** on the banks of the Ganga. The ruler was **Dhritarashtra**, a descendant of **Bharata,** the son of Dushyanta. He was one of the greatest Aryan kings. India is called Bharatvarsha, or the land of Bharata, after this great Aryan king.

Dhritarashtra had a hundred sons. They were called the **Kauravas.** He also had five nephews called the **Pandavas**. The eldest of the Pandavas was **Yudhishthira.** The second was **Bhima** who was known for his amazing strength. He ate great quantities of food and could uproot trees with his bare hands! **Arjuna,** the third brother, was a skillful archer and a brave warrior. The twins, **Nakula** and **Sahadeva** were the youngest.

Dhritarashtra loved the Pandavas like his own sons. He was now growing old, blind and weak. **Duryodhana** the eldest Kaurava was jealous of the five Pandavas, though they were his cousins. He kept harassing them and even tried to kill them. So the Pandavas left the palace and went away to seek their own fortune.

The neighbours of the Kauravas were the **Panchalas.** They were known for their valour and learning. The

The Archery Contest

Panchala king had a beautiful daughter called **Draupadi.** She was to choose herself a husband from among the most skillful warriors of the time. For this the king had arranged a contest.

The Pandavas, in their wandering, heard of this and decided to take part in the archery contest with many kings and princes.

The test was a difficult one. A great bow had to be lifted and an arrow shot through the eye of a golden fish by looking only at its reflection as it whirled above a great cauldron of oil. None of the princes present could match the skill of Arjuna. He won the contest and the hand of Draupadi.

With great delight the Pandavas returned home with Draupadi.

'Arjuna has won a great prize,' they called out to **Kunti,** their mother, who was inside the house.

'Share it among yourselves,' she shouted back, not knowing what the prize was.

The Pandavas could not disobey their mother and so Draupadi became the wife of all the five brothers!

The Pandavas now decided to return to Hastinapur. Dhritarashtra had missed them very much. He was sorry that they had to wander homeless for so long. He made up by giving them half of his kingdom.

Duryodhana had always hated the Pandavas. He was furious at what his father had done. He thought of a

wicked plan to snatch the kingdom from the Pandavas.

Duryodhana challenged Yudhishthira to a game of dice. In those days a king could not refuse such a challenge. Yudhishthira played and lost everything he had including his kingdom. He staked himself and his brothers. He lost again. Now all he had left was Draupadi. He staked her and lost her too. One of the Kauravas dragged her by the hair into the court. The Pandavas hung their heads in shame as the Kauravas rejoiced. Helpless, Draupadi prayed to **Lord Krishna** and was saved from disgrace.

Dhritarashtra could not bear to see what had happened. He gave back the Pandavas their kingdom. But the wicked Duryodhana would not leave them in peace. He challenged Yudhishthira to another game of dice. The stake this

time was very harsh. The losers had to spend twelve years in the forest and one more year in hiding without being found out. The Pandavas lost the game and went away to the forest with Draupadi.

The Pandavas spent the thirteen years in endless hardship. When they returned to Hastinapur, Duryodhana refused to give back their kingdom. Instead, he declared war on the Pandavas. They had no choice but to fight. The great battle, which was fought at a place called **Kurukshetra,** raged for eighteen days.

Many great warriors fought on each side. The Kaurava army was very large. The strength of the Pandava army was very small. But they fought with great valour. Lord Krishna was on their side and they were fighting for what was right. Finally, all the Kauravas were killed, the great army was defeated and Yudhishthira became king of Hastinapur.

This story is told in a great poem called the **Mahabharata.** It contains 100,000 verses and is the longest poem in the world. **Vyasa** was the sage who wrote the Mahabharata.

The most significant part of the Mahabharata is the sacred **Bhagavad Gita** or the Divine Song. It says that the

Krishna and Arjuna

most important thing is to do one's duty without worrying about the results. The best way for one to do his duty is to conquer selfishness and desire.

31

Kindness to All

A prince was born in the family of a **Vaishali** chief in 599 B.C. His name was **Vardhamana.**

Until about the age of thirty, Vardhamana led a life of comfort. He was married and had a daughter. But soon he left his home and family and went in search of knowledge. He roamed from place to place and faced many hardships.

After twelve years, when he was forty-two, he had a deep religious experience. He found what he had been looking for. He then came to be known as **Mahavira** or the great soul, and **Jina,** the Conquerer. He travelled far and wide sharing his ideas with others. His followers, the **Jainas** or as they became known as **Jains,** had conquered desire. They did this by severe discipline and fasting to the point of starvation.

Mahavira taught that everything in the universe, including trees, stones and even water has a soul. Man's main aim in life should be to make his soul pure. When that happens the soul is freed from the body and lives in happiness.

How can the soul be made pure? Not through knowledge, for no person can have total knowledge. He told the story of six blind men who were taken to an elephant. They were made to feel the different parts of its body and asked to guess what stood in front of them. The man who felt the elephant's tail said it was a huge snake, the one who felt its legs said it was a tree trunk, and so on. Similarly, an individual's knowledge can only be limited and not total.

'The soul can be made pure,' said Mahavira, 'by living a balanced life. A man must have right faith, right knowledge and right conduct.' By right conduct he meant not telling lies, not stealing, not injuring living beings and not being greedy. Extra wealth must be shared with others, by building hospitals for human beings as well as for animals and schools for children. The threefold virtues to be practised were called the three jewels or *tri-ratnas*.

Mahavira

Since everything has a soul, much care had to be taken to avoid killing even an ant. Jain monks went about with a muslin cloth over their mouths to avoid tiny insects from getting in by mistake and losing their lives. Jains avoided walking at night to avoid stepping on insects. This was the new teaching of **Ahimsa** or non-violence. It meant that no living thing should be hurt.

Mahavira spoke of a strict and simple life. Yet many people followed him and became Jains. He spoke out against the caste system. The teachings of Jainism became very popular among some people, particularly the traders and merchants. This was natural, since the other groups such as the Kshatriyas could hardly practise the vow of non-injury, just as the farmers could not avoid killing pests and insects.

Mahavira died at **Pawa,** in **Magadha**, at the age of seventy two. By then he had about 14,000 followers. Many more became Jains after that. About two hundred years after Mahavira's death which took place in 527 B.C. there was a great famine in north India. A Jain monk named **Bhadrabahu** left with a group of monks for the south. There they spread and followed Mahavira's teachings more strictly. They were called the **Digambaras** because they went about naked. The word Digambara means 'sky-clad'. The northern Jains are called **Svetambaras** or 'white-clothed'.

The Prince Who Gave Up His Throne

Lumbini is a beautiful place in the southern part of Nepal. Here, about 2,500 years ago, in 567 B.C. a baby boy was born to **Maya,** wife of **Shuddhodana**. Shuddhodana was the chief of the **Sakya** clan. **Kapilavastu** was his capital. The baby was named **Siddhartha.**

Siddhartha's mother died when he was only five days old. As the boy grew up, his father tried his best to keep Siddhartha happy. It is said that he had three palaces for three seasons built for his son. The little prince had everything he wanted — fine clothes, the best food and fascinating toys. But as he grew up, he became less and less fond of these things. What he liked most was to be alone so that he could think. His heart appeared troubled and uneasy.

When he was of age, he was married to a beautiful princess called **Yashodhara.** Soon they had a son whom they called **Rahula.** Even this did not cheer up the young prince.

One day, Siddhartha was driving through the streets in his royal chariot. He saw an old man, and then a sick man whose back was so bent that he could hardly walk. He could not understand why men should grow old or suffer. Then he saw a dead body being carried. He was very upset. His father had taken care that he did not see such sights inside the palace. He was shocked to see so much unhappiness in the world. For the first time he came to know that all men must indeed suffer, grow old and die.

As he was about to drive back into the palace, he saw a man in yellow robes, with a begging bowl in his hand. The prince was told that he was a monk who had given up the world to escape from the misery of his life. This man appeared most at

peace in the midst of the misery all about him. Siddhartha was very troubled. He decided that he would not rest until he found out why there was so much suffering in the world and how men could be free of it.

One night, while his wife slept with their little son in her arms, Siddhartha left his home. He went into the forest to search for a way out of suffering and sorrow, not just for himself but for all mankind. He knew that as long as he stayed at home enjoying the comforts of the palace he would never be able to find answers to his questions.

He spent some time with the hermits. He followed their way of life.

But they had no answers to his questions. Then for six years he denied himself all comfort and kept wandering from place to place. At last, he starved himself for forty days till his body seemed to be all bones. Five companions had kept him company all this while. Now, Siddhartha decided that fasting was of no use and gave it up. His companions were disgusted.

'He has given up the struggle they said and left him.

Now Siddhartha decided to think deeply about the things that disturbed

The Sights of Suffering

him. For forty-nine days he sat meditating under a **peepal** tree in **Bodh Gaya**. Then, suddenly, one day in the year 537 B.C., answers came to him. He felt as if he had learned all the secrets of the world. Buddha is one who has *bodhi* which means knowledge. Now that he had knowledge, Siddhartha, came to be known as the **Buddha**. The tree under which he sat is called the **Bodhi** tree.

What did Buddha find out? He found out that the world was full of sorrow and unhappiness. And the reason for it was greed and selfishness. Men wanted to have more and more things. How was one to end unhappiness?

Buddha said that to be free from suffering one must be free from greed and desire. Desire and worry and suffering came in various ways. From wanting a big house and then worrying in case it might be attacked by robbers; from wanting to be young and beautiful and feeling sad when wrinkles and grey hair appeared. To free himself from greed, man must follow the **Eight-fold Path.**

What is the eight-fold path? Right views, right resolve, right speech, right conduct, right livelihood, right effort, right recollection and right meditation. These will put an end to sorrow, suffering, hatred and anger and then mankind will have peace. Buddha also taught that all human

Buddha with Followers

beings were equal. There is no high or low, no Brahmin or Shudra.

'Not by birth does one become a Brahmin,' he said. 'Not by birth does one become a Shudra. But, by deeds one becomes a Brahmin. By deeds one becomes a Shudra.'

Buddha went from place to place, teaching people the truths he had found. His five companions had now returned to him. More and more people flocked to listen to him. One day he even went back to his family to share with them what he had found. Yashodhara and Rahula, who had now grown up, became his followers.

During this period the rules of the caste system had become very strict. Worship was no longer simple. Prayers were in Sanskrit which only the Brahmins understood. The teachings of Buddha spread far and wide and brought about changes in the country.

Buddha spoke in simple words and in **Prakrit,** a language ordinary people understood. All people were welcome to follow him. He loved everyone — king or shoe-maker, Brahmin or Shudra. Many times he refused invitations from rich people of high caste in order to be with the poor and needy. Buddha's life and teachings made all men feel that they were equal. Buddha died at the age of eighty in 487 B.C.

Many men and women followed Buddha's teachings in their day-to-day lives. Some became monks and nuns. They went from place to place spreading Buddha's teachings. Buddhism became very popular. Even kings became Buddhists. Buddhist monks and nuns spread the new religion beyond India's borders into countries such as, Sri Lanka, China, Japan, Burma, Bhutan and Tibet.

Porus and Alexander

During the time when Buddha and Mahavira were preaching their new religions, India was made up of a number of small kingdoms. A powerful king named **Cyrus** ruled in **Persia,** now known as Iran. He crossed the **Hindukush** mountains and conquered the Indus valley. A large area of India now became a province of the Persian empire. The capital of this province was **Taxila,** which soon became a great centre of learning. As a result of the Persian conquest, new types of gold and silver coins and a new type of script were introduced into India. This part of India remained with the Persians for about two hundred years.

Then, in far off **Macedon** (Greece) there rose a powerful young king, **Alexander.** He dreamt of conquering the whole world. At the age of twenty-six, starting out with an army of 30,000 men, he conquered the whole of

Alexander

Syria, Palestine, Egypt and Persia in just four years. Strong and proud after so many great victories, in 326 B.C. he crossed the Hindukush mountains and entered the Punjab. Soon he found out that there were two powerful kings in the Punjab — **Ambhi** and **Porus**.

Ambhi, the raja of Taxila, did not fight but welcomed Alexander with presents. He also offered to supply him with 5,000 soldiers. Alexander was very pleased.

He now ordered Porus, 'Come to Taxila and pay homage to me.'

'I will certainly meet you,' replied Porus, 'not at Taxila but on the borders of my own kingdom and at the head of a large army!'

Porus was as good as his word. He camped with his army on the right bank of the river **Jhelum**. Alexander's army was on the opposite side. Jhelum was in flood. At night as it rained heavily, Alexander marched upstream till he came to a sharp bend in the river. Here he crossed the river with his horses in chest-deep water. There was a sudden attack on the camp of Porus. Porus' army was slow in fighting back. Their chariots got stuck in the mud and the soldiers took shelter behind the elephants. The wounded elephants were frightened and ran amok, trampling both the enemy and their own soldiers. Porus himself fought bravely but by evening it was all over. Almost fainting from the pain of several wounds and loss of blood, he surrendered. He was brought in chains to Alexander.

'How shall I treat you?' asked Alexander with the pride of a conquerer.

'Like a king!' replied the equally proud Porus.

Alexander liked Porus for his courage and self-respect. He ordered him to be released at once and gave back his kingdom.

Alexander now marched on with his sight on other kingdoms. He crossed three more rivers and came up to the banks of the Beas. Here his soldiers refused to go any further because they were tired and homesick. Alexander had no choice but to return home. He sent half his army by sea and the other half he took with him along the coast. He never reached Macedon. He died at Babylon, in 323 B.C. at the age of 33.

Our knowledge about Alexander's invasion of India is from the accounts of Greeks who accompanied him. They wrote down what they saw. They have described the climate, plants and crops of India. They have also written in detail about the religion and customs of the people. Many Greeks even stayed back and made their homes in India. New trade routes were opened between north-west India and the west. Trade increased and there was an exchange of not only goods but also of ideas.

Porus before Alexander

Chandragupta and Chanakya

Mauryan Coins

Taxila in northwest India was a great city known for trade and learning. Gifted young men from far and wide went there to complete their education. Here gurus or teachers taught them religion, philosophy, mathematics, medicine and astronomy. In the fourth century B.C. **Panini**, the most learned scholar from Taxila wrote the grammar of the Sanskrit language.

When Alexander left India, he appointed Greek governors to look after the territories he had conquered. With his sudden death the governors too left. There was disorder and confusion in the north-west. An adventurous young man had been watching the events very closely. His name was **Chandragupta Maurya.** He too had dreams of becoming a conqueror like Alexander. He thought that the time was ripe to realize his dream.

Magadha (south Bihar) was a powerful kingdom in north India. It was ruled by a king named **Dhana Nanda**. Chandragupta, who belonged to the **Moriya** tribe, had once been a general in the king's army. For some reason the king happened to be annoyed with him and expelled Chandragupta from the kingdom. He wandered about in the Punjab biding

41

Eat from the sides

his time.

Soon, he met a very clever Brahmin named **Kautilya**, also known as **Chanakya.** Now Kautilya too had been in the court of Dhana Nanda. He had left Magadha because the king had insulted him and had vowed to avenge himself. The two became friends and plotted together to take revenge. Kautilya taught Chandragupta how to become a strong king. Chandragupta began to collect an army. He first attacked the leaderless kingdoms of the northwest which had been deserted by the Greek governors. Having brought a large area under his control, he marched towards Magadha.

Magadha was a vast and powerful kingdom. It was not easy to capture it all at once. It is said that once Chandragupta saw a mother scolding her child for eating from the centre of the plate. 'It's far too hot there,' she warned, 'you'll burn your mouth. Eat from the sides of the dish where the food is cooler.'

'That's it!' said Chandragupta, as an idea flashed his mind. 'Now I know how to defeat Magadha. I shall attack from the edges of the kingdom first, then move slowly in towards the capital, **Pataliputra.**' His plan worked. With his small army he managed to capture the great kingdom of Magadha. He was crowned the king of Magadha in 321 B.C. Soon the whole of north India was firmly under his control.

Now, **Seleukos,** one of Alexander's generals, had become the master of most of the kingdoms Alexander had conquered. He wanted to include even Punjab into his territory. With a large army Seleukos marched into the Punjab. Chandragupta met him in battle and defeated him. He was forced to give

Chandragupta not only a large part of Afghanistan, but also his daughter in marriage.

Later, when there was peace between them, Seleukos sent an ambassador to Pataliputra. His name was **Megasthenes.** He wrote a book called **Indika,** in which he described all he saw during his stay here. Kautilya also wrote a book titled **Arthashastra.** From these two books we gather a lot about the times of Chandragupta Maurya.

Chandragupta's kingdom grew larger with every conquest and became a great empire. Chandragupta with the help of his clever minister Kautilya, ruled his land well. He lived in a grand palace surrounded by a group of armed women.

Pataliputra (Patna) was a large city, with many beautiful parks and ponds and houses two or three storeys high. It was surrounded by a great wall which had more than 500 watch-towers. Many foreigners lived in Pataliputra and the king set up a separate department to look after their affairs.

The king undertook many activities for the welfare of the people. Dams and canals were built to bring water to dry areas. There were hospitals to take care of the sick. Roads were built linking important cities. There was a wide road connecting **Purushpura** (Peshawar) and Pataliputra. It was more than 1,900 kilometres long. There were shady trees on either side and every few kilometres there were rest houses.

Some ancient Jain books tell us that towards the end of his reign, Chandragupta became a Jain. He handed his throne over to his son and accompanied by some Jain monks went to **Sravana Belagola** in south India. There he died a peaceful death.

Chandragupta meets Chanakya

43

The Royal Monk

Ashoka Pillar

Chandragupta's son was **Bindusara.** Very little is known about him. He must have been an able king and a great general, for by the end of his rule, the Mauryan kingdom included the whole of India, except for the extreme southern part and **Kalinga** (Orissa) in the east. This was the first real Indian empire and Ashoka, the son of Bindusara, inherited it around 272 B.C.

Ashoka, during the first few years of his reign, lived like any other powerful king. He decided that he ought to make his empire bigger and stronger and so he attacked Kalinga with a mighty army. The people of Kalinga fought bravely. It was a fierce battle. A hundred thousand men were killed and many times that number died of their wounds. The people of Kalinga were completely crushed.

However, the victory did not make Ashoka happy. He was horrified at the destruction and suffering he had caused. He vowed never to use his sword again. 'The drums of war shall never be beaten in my land again,' he proclaimed.

Ashoka was drawn to the gentle teaching of Buddha and became a Buddhist. He gave up hunting and killing. He led a pure and good life and urged his people to do the same.

Ashoka's empire was so vast that he could not meet and talk to his people himself. So he thought of an excellent plan. He got his messages carved on pillars of stone and put them up in every corner of the country. These writings or **edicts** as they are called, were in **Pali,** the language which the people spoke. They asked people to be kind, truthful and gentle. They also tell us about the greatness of Ashoka.

'All men are my children,' he says in one of the edicts. 'In truth the king, beloved of the gods, has at heart security for subjects, respect for life, peace and happiness.'

He visited all the places connected with Buddha's life. He put up a pillar to mark the place where Buddha was born. He built many **viharas,** or places where Buddhist holy men could live. In fact, he built so many of these that Magadha came to be known as the country of viharas or Bihar, as it is called today.

One of Ashoka's pillars is at **Sarnath,** near Varanasi. On top it has the figure of four lions sitting back to back. This forms the official seal of the Indian government today. Another symbol often seen in Ashoka's edicts is a wheel. He had ruled his country not by force but

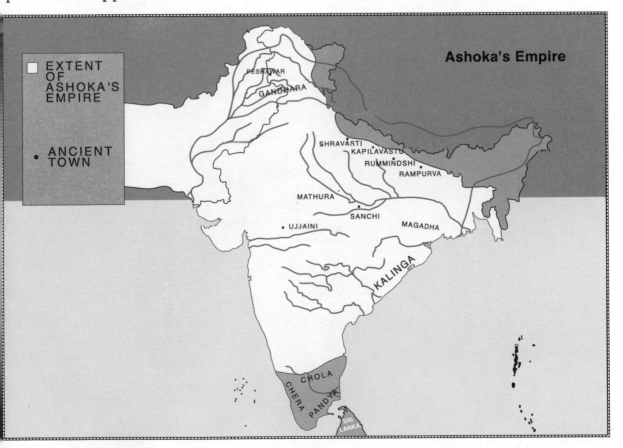

EXTENT OF ASHOKA'S EMPIRE

• ANCIENT TOWN

Ashoka's Empire

PESHAWAR
GANDHARA
SHRAVASTI
KAPILAVASTU
RUMMINDSHI
RAMPURVA
MATHURA
SANCHI
• UJJAINI
MAGADHA
KALINGA
CHOLA
CHERA
PANDYA
SRI LANKA

according to *dhamma* or the law of piety. The wheel stands for *dhamma*.

Though Ashoka was a Buddhist, he did not force his views on the people following other beliefs. Instead he encouraged and helped them to practise their own religions. He asked his governors to think of themselves as 'good nurses' and not to be violent, harsh, impatient or idle.

Ashoka himself went on tours to see for himself the living conditions of the people. He had trees planted, wells dug, rest houses and hospitals built for people and animals alike. He stopped the killing of animals for food or sacrifice. By his own example and guidance Ashoka tried to bring peace among many different groups of people that lived within his large kingdom. For these reasons he is considered the greatest king India has ever known.

Ashoka called a great **Buddhist Council** at Pataliputra to resolve the differences that had arisen in the community of monks. At this council it was decided to send some holy and learned men to the neighbouring countries. The group to **Sri Lanka** was led by Ashoka's son, **Mahendra.** He carried with him a branch of the Bodhi tree. The king of Sri Lanka and many of his subjects became Buddhists. Ashoka died about the year 232 B.C.

A Vihara

46

The Empire Breaks up

Menander

Ashoka had held together a great empire for 37 years. When he died, it began to break up into many small kingdoms. Kalinga, which had been conquered by Ashoka was the first to break away and the others followed. In the end, Mauryan kings were left ruling only the **Gangetic** plain. Then one day, the last Mauryan king **Brihadratha** was killed by his own general **Pushyamitra Sunga.**

The whole of northwestern India had fallen into the hands of foreigners. There were as many as 39 Indo-Greek kings and two Greek queens ruling over little kingdoms. And their rule lasted over a hundred years.

One of the Indo-Greek kings was **Menander.** He was a man of many interests. He seems to have been a very popular king. His capital was

Sakala (Sialkot). Its streets hummed with activity with people of different faiths going about their business in peace. The king was open to new ideas. He's said to have once had a discussion with the Buddhist scholar **Nagasena**. He was so impressed by Nagasena's wisdom that he became a follower of Buddha.

Just as the Greeks had forced their way into India, now others began to arrive. The **Shakas** came first, followed by the **Pahlavas** towards the end of the first century B.C. Then came more tribes from the western borders of China. This happened about the time that **Jesus Christ** was born.

One of the tribes that came was called the **Kushanas**. They were originally nomads who had once lived on the border of China. They were pushed out of their areas by a stronger tribe called the **Huns**. On entering India they defeated the Shakas and the Pahlavas and settled down in Afghanistan and Kashmir.

Their greatest king was **Kanishka**. He was a capable general. He won many battles and added many new areas to his kingdom. His kingdom stretched from Central Asia to the borders of Bengal. It included Punjab, Kashmir, Sindh and Gujarat. His capital was Peshawar.

Kushana Coins

The Headless Statue of Kanishka

48

Kanishka came in contact with a great Buddhist scholar called **Ashvaghosha.** The king heard from him the many wonderful things Buddha had taught and became his follower. He tried to spread Buddha's teachings among his subjects. Soon Buddhist monasteries, **stupas** and temples came up in Bactria, Afghanistan, Gandhara, Kashmir and Punjab. The whole of the northwest began to look like a Buddhist holy land.

About this time the idea of one God who cared and loved his people was growing strong. In West Asia, Jesus had helped spread this thought and many people had accepted Jesus as their saviour. **St. Thomas,** one of Christ's disciples is believed to

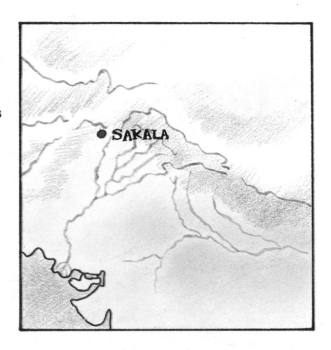

have brought the teachings of Jesus to India. After preaching the new religion along the **Malabar** coast he moved east and was killed by angry local residents while he was saying his prayers. Today, a beautiful church stands in Chennai, where he is believed to have been killed.

During the reign of the Kushanas trade, both within and outside the country, continued to grow and expand. The borders of the **Roman** empire in the west and India were only about 900 kilometres apart. There were trade routes between Rome and India both over land and sea. Romans bought spices, indigo, pearls, jewels, perfumes and muslin from India. India received gold in return.

Kushana Sculpture

The Satavahanas

The three earliest kingdoms of south India were the **Pandya,** the **Chola** and the **Chera.** These had lasted for several years. The Pandyas had such a great army that even Megasthenes, who visited the court of Chandragupta Maurya from far-off Greece had heard about it. Chera kings conducted trade with West Asia by the sea route. Their ships took spices and pearls and brought back gold. The Cheras were also known for their rich merchants.

When the Maurya empire was breaking up the **Satavahanas** were carving out a kingdom for themselves in the south. The Satavahanas or **Andhras** had formerly been local officials under the Mauryas. They ruled for four hundred years from about 225 B.C. to A.D. 225 At one time their empire stretched right across the middle of the country, from the Arabian Sea to the Bay of Bengal, from the Deccan to the mouth of the Krishna river and included Kathiawar, Gujarat and Malwa in the north.

The Satavahanas helped bring the people of the north and south closer. There were both Hindus and Buddhists in their kingdom. Some excellent Buddhist buildings were built during their rule. The most

Carvings

50

The Stupa at Sanchi

famous of these is at **Sanchi.** Here an old Ashokan stupa was enlarged to twice its original size. It was surrounded by a railing which had four gateways facing the four main directions. The railings and gateways were carved with scenes from Buddha's life. There were scenes crowded with animals, trees, flowers and people and appeared to be bursting with life.

A large number of Buddhist temples and monasteries too were constructed during this period, most of them carved out of rocks in the hillsides. Some of these can be seen even today at places such as **Bhaja, Kanheri** and **Karle**. Work on the famous **Ajanta** caves first started at the time of the Satavahana kings.

The viharas or monasteries are square chambers surrounded by little rooms meant for the monks. The **chaityas** or temples are rectangular in shape with a semi-circular end in which a stupa is placed. Along the walls are rows of pillars, often, intricately carved with groups of horses and elephants with their riders.

The Satavahana kings traded with other kingdoms. Goods meant for these countries were brought to **Kalyan,** near modern Bombay and shipped out. The merchants involved in this export business became so rich that some of them built massive cave temples with their own money.

Satavahana Kingdom

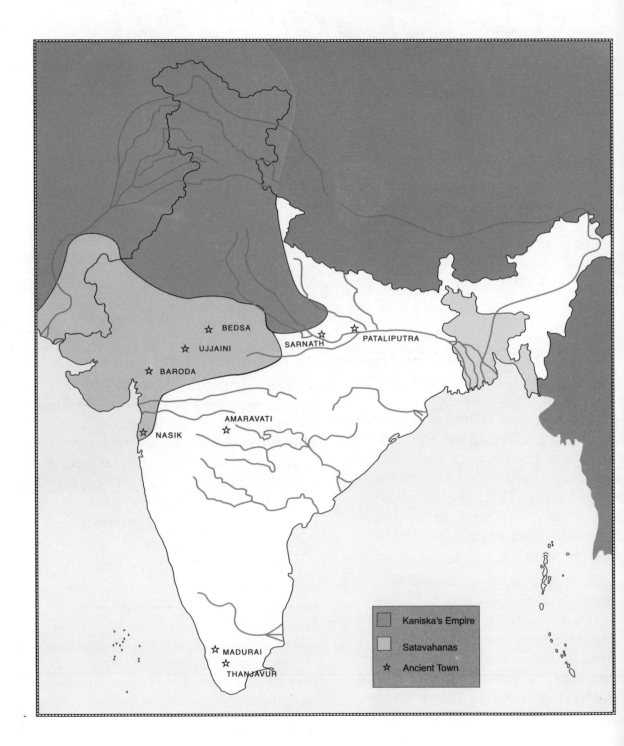

The Gupta Empire

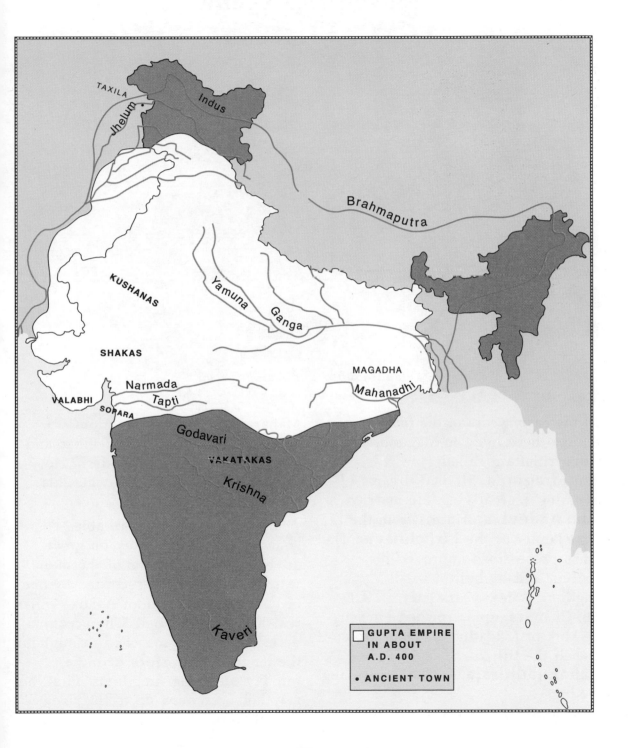

TAXILA

Indus

Jhelum

Brahmaputra

KUSHANAS

Yamuna

Ganga

SHAKAS

MAGADHA

VALABHI

Narmada

Tapti

Mahanadhi

SOPARA

Godavari

VAKATAKAS

Krishna

Kaveri

GUPTA EMPIRE IN ABOUT A.D. 400

● ANCIENT TOWN

The Emperor Who
Played the Veena

Chandragupta and Kumaradevi

In the early years of the fourth century there lived in Magadha a young chieftain called **Chandragupta.** He had dreams of becoming a great king. He married **Kumaradevi**, a princess from the royal family of the **Lichchhavis**. The wife's possessions improved his position and he built a small kingdom. A few years later, in A.D 320, Chandragupta crowned himself the king of Magadha and took upon himself the title of **Maharajadhiraja** — The Great King of Kings.

Though he called himself Maharajadhiraja, his kingdom was small. It consisted only of Bihar and parts of eastern Uttar Pradesh. He ruled till about A.D. 335 when his son **Samudragupta** took over.

Samudragupta was an able general. He led his army on great adventures. The details of the many wars he fought were recorded by one of his court poets on an Ashoka pillar which is at Allahabad. The account describes how he marched throughout the length and breadth of India, forcibly annexing kingdoms. First, he marched westward up to the river Chambal and then eastward as far as

Kalinga. His greatest adventure was a brilliant march into south India. He marched along the eastern coast up to **Kanchipuram,** near Chennai, covering a distance of over 1,900 kilometres. He then moved westward and made his long way back to Pataliputra.

Altogether, he led his armies over 4,800 kilometres and did not suffer a single defeat. He brought eleven kings under his authority and made them pay large quantities of gold and jewels.

He celebrated his triumphs by performing the *Ashwamedha Yagna* — the ancient horse sacrifice. No one dared to stop the horse Samudragupta sent and so he proclaimed himself Emperor.

Samudragupta was not just a general who fought wars. He was an extremely talented man. He wrote poetry and held discussions with learned men. He was fond of music. Some of his coins show him sitting with a *veena* in his hands.

Samudragupta had indeed headed a truly great empire — great not only in size, but also in achievements. After a gap of several years India was, once again, united as one country. His rule was efficient and gentle. The country was prosperous and the people were generally happy. The study of art, literature and science flourished. Samudragupta's name spread far and wide. The king

of Sri Lanka sent ambassadors to his court. They were received with honour and given permission to build a Buddhist monastery at Bodh Gaya.

Mahabodhi Temple, Bodhgaya

Vikramaditya

Vikramaditya

The greatest of the Gupta kings was, perhaps, Samudragupta's son Chandragupta. He later gave himself the title of **Vikramaditya,** which means the *Son of Valour*. He indeed, turned out to be so when he made the Gupta Empire larger and stronger than ever before. The most important battle he fought was against the **Sakas** of **Malwa.** The Saka ruler was killed and his kingdom was taken over.

His victory over the lands in the west gave him control over sea-ports such as Surat and Broach. These were the main centres of trade with Europe. In the north he conquered parts of northern Afghanistan and appointed a governor in Kashmir. In the south he married a **Vakataka** princess and gained control over their state.

During Vikramaditya's rule, a Chinese pilgrim **Fa Hien** visited India. Fa Hien spent 11 years in India studying Sanskrit and visiting holy places. He wrote down what he saw during his travels.

'The people', he wrote, 'are prosperous and happy. They are kind to one another and have very good

government his hands were cut off. But this was very rare.

Young men and women were expected to know how to dance, sing and play musical instruments. Vikramaditya's court was full of musicians, poets, artists and writers. The king had chosen nine of the best and called them *navaratnas* (nine gems). It is believed that the great poet **Kalidasa** was one of them. He wrote in Sanskrit. **Shakuntala** is his most famous play. It has been translated into several languages of the world and is staged even today. **Raghuvansa** and **Meghdoot** are the two most famous poems of Kalidasa.

Sanskrit was the court language. Many books were written in Sanskrit on subjects such as philosophy, law, drama, dance, painting and architecture. Teaching was done only in Sanskrit. Some of the most beautiful buildings and statues were built during this time. Hindu gods were often shown with four or even eight arms. Hindus built temples imitating the Buddhists in carving them out of hillsides. At Ajanta, Buddhist and Hindu temples can be found side by side. Some of the more famous paintings of Ajanta belong to the Gupta period.

Vikramaditya was succeeded by his son, **Kumaragupta,** in A.D. 415 and then by **Skandagupta.** The Gupta kings ruled for about 160 years.

manners.'

In Magadha there were rest houses where people could eat and rest. There were hospitals which treated the sick free of cost. There were also hospitals for animals. People were generally kind to animals and very few killed them for food. The government hardly interfered with the lives of people. They could move about freely in any part of the country. There was no death penalty. Generally people were fined according to the seriousness of the offence. If a person rebelled against the

Herbal Remedies and Plastic Surgery

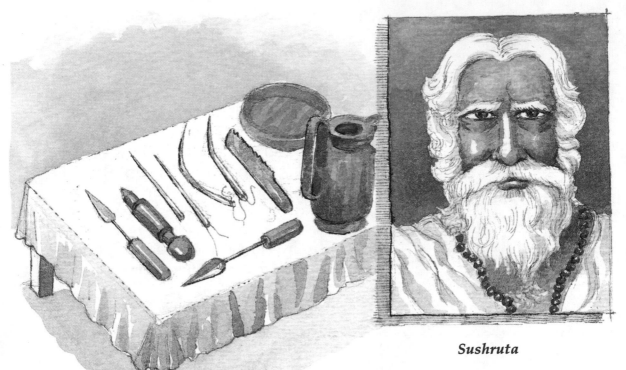

Surgical Instruments

Sushruta

What is known as plastic surgery was practised as long back as the first century A.D. by **Sushruta.** He not only conducted surgical operations but also wrote about them. His book, the *Sushruta Samhita* was based on the teachings of **Dhanvantari,** who lived much earlier. It deals with surgery as well as medicine. The book describes five types of bones, eight kinds of operations, fourteen types of bandages and 121 surgical instruments! Sushruta insisted that before operating, surgeons should shave off their beards, clip their nails, take a bath and wear clean white clothes. He expected patients to drink wine before an operation, as it would help lessen their pain.

Aryabhata the great astronomer and mathematician lived during the Gupta period. He was convinced that it was really the earth that was moving and not the stars. He believed that the earth had an invisible axis through its centre and that it rotated on this axis like a ball. The other astronomers of his time had believed that the earth was the centre of the

One of the oldest medical textbooks, the *Charaka Samhita* was partly written by **Charaka** during the reign of Emperor Kanishka. Charaka had done excellent work in the field of healing and medicine. He gave great importance to medicines made from herbs.

The *Charaka Samhita* has eight

Charaka

Aryabhata

olar system, and that the sun, the moon, and the stars revolved around the earth. Aryabhata's value for, π or pi' of 3.1416, is still used today. The great scholar delighted in challenging popular beliefs and arriving at correct explanations for things.

sections and is divided into a 150 chapters. It lists over six hundred drugs that come from plants, minerals, and animals. The book also lays down guidelines for those in the medical profession. Among other things it says, 'a doctor must not betray his patients, even at the cost of his own life.'

Terror Strikes!

Something dreadful happened to India during the rule of Skandagupta. Fierce nomads called the **Huns** from Central Asia, invaded India from the northwest.

The Huns were excellent horsemen. They could stay on horseback for days together and it is said they could even sleep on horseback! They were good marksmen too who never missed their target with a spear or an arrow. They lived in tents made of skins, ate uncooked meat and drank sour milk. They were like hungry lions waiting for someone to devour.

The Huns came as if in waves, thousands of them. Skandagupta managed to repel them for a while but, they could not be stopped for long. Hardly had one wave been pushed back when another would appear through the mountain passes. By and by they crossed Punjab, Rajasthan, Kathiawar and went as far as Bihar. And wherever they went, they looted and burned houses, killed people and took away everything they could lay their hands on. They would stop for the night at the place they had looted and then be off again the next morning on their trail of destruction. There was no one to stop them.

After a while, **Toramana**, the leader of the Huns, declared himself king. He made Shakala his capital. His reign was one of cruelty and terror. People obeyed him because they were afraid of him. But secretly they hated him and wished his reign would end. Toramana's son **Mihiragula** was even more wicked than his father. For 70 years the people of the region lived in misery and fear.

The attacks of the Huns had greatly reduced the strength of the Guptas. After Skandagupta's death, the Gupta kings held on to Magadha for some time. But by about A.D. 550. the Gupta empire crumbled into a number of small states. The whole of north India plunged into confusion. Petty rival kings fought among themselves for power and territory.

The King Who Gave Away his Riches

The king of **Thaneshwar,** near Kurukshetra, was **Prabhakara-vardhana.** He had three children: two sons named **Rajya** and **Harsha,** and a daughter named **Rajyasri.** Rajyasri, at 13 was married to the ruler of **Kanauj.** In the year A.D.655 the king fell seriously ill and died.

Rajya, the eldest son became king. But soon news came from Kanauj that Rajyasri's husband had been killed in a battle with the king of Malwa and Rajyasri herself had been taken prisoner. Rajya marched quickly towards Kanauj but was killed in a plot by another king called **Sasanka.**

Harsha was just 16 years old then. Without any delay, he put himself at the head of the army and marched against the king of Malwa. He fought with great courage, routed his enemy and rescued his sister.

The people of Kanauj who had seen Harsha on the battlefield, and who were without a king, now, requested Harsha to be their king. Harsha agreed and was crowned king of the combined states of Kanauj and Thaneshwar.

The trouble faced by his brother and brother-in-law, showed Harsha the danger posed by other kings to his kingdom. He decided to conquer

Harsha on the March

his neighbours and strengthen his own kingdom. For six years Harsha fought battle after battle. His elephants were always in harness and his soldiers never took off their armour. At the end of six years he had won over most of north India. His kingdom, now, extended from the Himalayas to the river Narmada. Then, he tried to cross the Narmada and extend his territory into south

61

India. But there was a powerful king called **Pulakesin** in the Deccan. He defeated Harsha and forced him to go back.

A writer called **Bana** lived at the king's court. He was also the king's close friend. He wrote a book called **Harshacharita.** It gives a good account of Harsha's rule.

His kingdom was large but loosely put together. Most parts were governed by rulers whom Harsha had defeated in war. Harsha supervised their work by going on long tours to different parts of the country. He looked into the collection of taxes, listened to complaints and examined the records. Camps of bamboo and reed were put up wherever he chose to halt. People were encouraged to meet him directly with their problems. Officials did not receive money as salary but were given land to cultivate. One-sixth of the crop grown was paid to the king as tax and the rest retained as salary.

We know a lot about Harsha's times from yet another person. He is **Hiuen Tsang,** a Chinese pilgrim, who spent about 15 years in India. Though he came to study Buddhism and to visit holy places, he took a keen interest in other matters.

When he arrived at Kanauj, Harsha was on a tour. When Harsha heard of his arrival he sent word that he should come to his camp. Hiuen Tsang arrived at the camp one late evening. Since it was dark he pitched his camp on the river bank, hoping to meet the king the next morning. The king was camping on the other side of the river.

Harsha Giving away his Riches

62

In the middle of the night suddenly there was a loud beating of the drums. The dark river was lit up with torches. Hiuen Tsang woke up in great alarm. He was told that the king was coming to see him. Harsha was so keen to meet the learned man from China that he would not wait till morning!

Harsha and Rajyasri met the Chinese visitor and were delighted. In the days that followed they had many discussions. And by the time they returned to Kanauj they had both accepted Buddhism.

Though he became a Buddhist, Harsha continued to pray to Shiva and the sun, like other Hindus. He respected all religions. And the kindness and generosity he practised was rarely seen before. Every five years he went to **Prayag** and gave away to Buddhists, Jains, Hindus, the poor and the needy all he had — money, jewels and clothes. It is said that once he had to borrow an old garment from his sister to cover himself, as he had nothing to wear!

Hiuen Tsang had written everything down just as he had seen and heard. Harsha's rule was gentle and taxes were light. He was sincerely concerned about the welfare of the people. His people were happy and life was pleasant. Like other great kings before him, he erected rest houses and built hospitals for people and animals. He also spent a great

Hiuen Tsang

amount of money on building and supporting Buddhist monasteries.

Education was of a very high standard. The Buddhist **University of Nalanda** was so famous that students from as far as Tibet, China and Korea came to study there. There were tough entrance examinations to pass to get admission. Students studied subjects such as grammar, medicine, mathematics, philosophy and, of course, religion. The university had an enormous library that spread over three buildings. There was strict discipline. For a grave fault a student could be expelled.

Harsha died in A.D. 647 but as he had left no heir, his empire soon collapsed. Northern India once again broke up into several big and small kingdoms.

Kings of the South

When Harshavardhana was ruling the north there were three important kingdoms in the south. The Deccan was ruled by the early **Chalukyas** of **Badami**. The far south was ruled by both the **Pallavas** of **Kanchi** and the **Pandyas** of **Madurai**.

The greatest of the Chalukya kings was **Pulakesin II**. He ruled during the same period as Harsha. Hiuen Tsang had visited his kingdom and found the land rich and the people hardworking. The king was an able ruler. His subjects obeyed and respected him. The king's fame had spread far and wide. That he received ambassadors from the king of Persia is recorded in one of the paintings in the Ajanta caves.

Pulakesin was so powerful that he defeated Harsha and stopped him from entering the south. He also fought and defeated the Pallava king **Mahendravarman I** and took away some of his lands.

The Pallavas, who ruled from Kanchipuram, were the first really important Tamil kings. In the early seventh century their king was Mahendravarman I. Though defeated by Pulakesin in war, he was a talented person in other fields. He was a writer and encouraged many scholars and poets to visit his court.

Originally a Jain, he later became a Hindu. Some famous rock temples in **Mahabalipuram,** near Chennai, were carved during his reign.

During the reign of the Pallavas, Kanchipuram became a great educational and religious centre. In the city was a great university. Over the centuries Kanchipuram also became a temple city with over one thousand temples built there.

Narasimhavarman who succeeded Mahendravarman was a more capable general than his father. He defeated Pulakesin II, after which, the Chalukyas gradually became weak. In A.D. 753, the **Rashtrakutas** took over from the Chalukyas. The Pallavas lasted for a hundred years more, when they were overthrown by the **Cholas** of **Tanjore**.

The Rashtrakuta king **Krishna I**

is remembered as the one who built the great **Kailasha** temple at **Ellora.** This magnificient temple is considered one of the greatest buildings in the history of mankind. Another important Rashtrakuta king was **Amoghavarsha I**. During his reign the Rashtrakutas became powerful and by the tenth century A.D. their kingdom stretched from sea to sea, from Malwa in the north to Kanchi in the south.

The Cholas who ended the Pallava rule became very powerful in the far

A 6th/7th Century Temple

south. Their power reached its height under **Rajaraja I** and his son **Rajendra.** Both of them fought several wars and added new territories to their kingdom. They kept a powerful navy and attacked the **Maldive** islands, Sri Lanka and the **Shrivijaya** kingdom in Southeast Asia and won many important battles as far as Malaya and Sumatra. Their main aim was to protect their trade between India and China.

Rajendra Chola defeated the **Pala** kings of Bengal and called himself 'the Chola who brought the Ganga south'. He also built dams, lakes and canals so that the farmers of his kingdom might always have water for their fields. The artisans in the Chola kingdom made beautiful bronze images most of which are now preserved in museums. The most famous among them is of the dancing Shiva. The great **Shiva** temple at **Tanjore** was built by Rajaraja Chola.

The Cheras, whose rule extended to the Malabar coast welcomed traders from abroad. Under the Cheras, trade grew rapidly with Persia and Arabia in the west, and China in the east. Textiles, spices, medicines, jewels and ivory were exported. Horses were the main item imported.

There were changes taking place in the life of the people too. Ideas and practices from the north spread to the south. The people of the south accepted some and rejected others. Some they changed and made their own. The caste system entered their life and became firmly established.

Temples occupied a central place in the life of the people. The village assembly was held there and so was the school. Many people were employed in the temples. Singing and dancing were a regular part of temple life

Shilappadigaram (The Jewelled Anklet) is a famous Tamil poem

written around the sixth century A.D. It is a long story like the 'Mahabharata'. But unlike the 'Mahabharata', it is a story not of princes and wars but of ordinary people with ordinary problems. Today, **Kannagi**, the heroine of the story is honoured as a goddess by all faithful wives.

The Sea Trade

One of the most fascinating things about the life of the people was **local self-government.** The villages were governed by the villagers themselves. They collected taxes, settled disputes and looked after education and farming. There was a village **headman** and he was helped by a village **assembly.**

67

Holy Men of the South

Sankara

When so many events were taking place around them some people began to think about religion too. People did not like some of the ideas that had crept into the Hindu religion. The men and women who tried to purify their religion were called **Alvars** and **Nayanars.** They travelled from place to place composing hymns and singing them before the images of their gods. They believed that God was everywhere. He could be approached only through *bhakti* or love. Since God is in everyone, all men are equal. Love of God was to be shown in loving one's fellowmen.

Another great movement that began in the south was in the field of **Philosophy.** In the eighth century a great man was born in Kerala. His name was **Sankara.** He studied the Upanishads and other holy books with great interest. He began asking questions such as: What is the world? What is God? Who am I?

He set out from home, visiting places, meeting people and spreading his teachings. When people did not agree with him he would argue and try to make them understand. He wrote many books on philosophy and composed devotional poems. Sankara's teachings made Hinduism once again the most important religion in India.

Sankara established four *maths* in four corners of India: **Badrinath** in the north, **Puri** in the east, **Dwarka** in the west and **Shringeri** in the south. A large number of pilgrims started visiting these places and they became centres of Hindu learning.

The teaching of Sankaracharya soon spread across the length and breadth of the country. But not all thinkers would accept what he taught. In the eleventh century, a Tamil Brahmin named **Ramanuja** taught that *bhakti* or love and devotion was a better way to reach God than just knowledge. The Supreme God according to him was Vishnu. Out of love, he could forgive sins and draw us to himself. Ramanuja's teachings were similar to those of the Tamil saints but he insisted on observing the caste system.

The great thinkers and Brahmins taught in Sanskrit. It was the language of the universities as well as of the royal courts in the south. Some great Sanskrit books were written during this period.

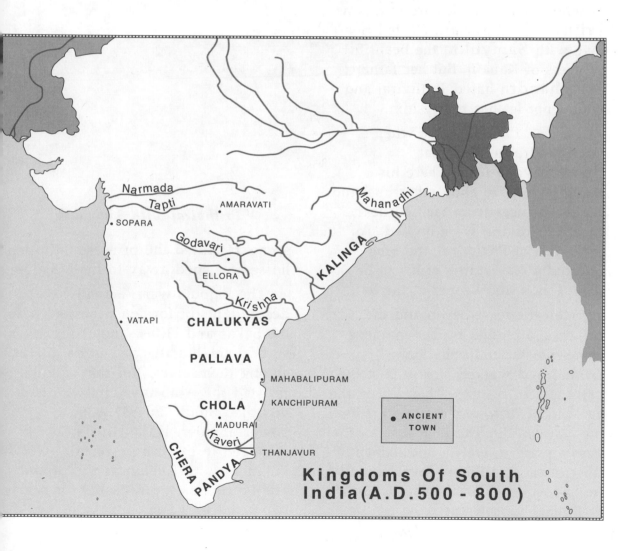

Kingdoms Of South India (A.D. 500 - 800)

The Valiant Rajputs

About the time that Sankaracharya lived, a family of Rajput kings called the **Pratiharas** became powerful in the north. Their kingdoms stretched from Bihar in the east to Kathiawar on the west coast.

One of the famous Rajput kings, of whom many stories are told, was **Prithviraj Chauhan.** He fell in love with **Samyukta** the beautiful princess of Kanauj. But her father **Jayachandra** hated Prithviraj and would not let her marry him.

At last, the day came when Jayachandra held a great **Swayamvara** feast where his daughter was to choose her husband. All the princes from far and near, except Prithviraj were invited. To make fun of Prithviraj, the king ordered a clay statue of his to be placed as a doorkeeper at the hall.

Soon the feast began and the princess, attended by her maidens came into the hall. She looked around and walked slowly past the gathering of princes. Then lifting the garland of flowers she placed it on the clay statue! The king and all the guests present, would not believe their eyes. And before Jayachandra could recover from the shock, Prithviraj himself appeared on the

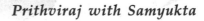

Prithviraj with Samyukta

scene. He lifted the princess on to his horse and sped away to his kingdom.

The Rajputs were, actually, the descendants of foreign tribes, such as the Sakas and Huns. They ruled over several small states and often fought among themselves. But they also resisted the Arab invaders who had occupied Sindh. In A.D. 836 a powerful ruler, **Raja Bhoja,** managed to build a powerful kingdom with Kanauj as the capital. The Pratihara empire lasted for nearly two hundred years. But the many

vars they had to fight gradually
made them weak.

Among the other Rajput families
that ruled in the north were the
Paramars of Malwa, the **Chandelas**
of Bundelkhand, the **Solankis** of
Gujarat and the **Chauhans** of Ajmer.

The Rajputs had developed a way
of life of their own. They loved
nothing better than war. From an
early age children were taught riding,
shooting and other battle skills. The
poets sang songs of heroic deeds of
ancestors and encouraged people to be
brave.

Rajput women too were taught to
be brave. They did not hesitate to go
into the battlefield if need arose.
Rajputs preferred to die rather than be
dishonoured. If a Rajput king was
killed in war, it was the custom of all
the ladies of the court to commit
Jauhar (burn themselves to death)
rather than be captured by the enemy.

Besides the Rajputs, there were
several other kingdoms in the north.
There were the kingdoms of Punjab,
Kashmir and Assam. The **Palas**, who
were Buddhists, ruled in Bengal.
They had ships which sailed to
Malaya and other countries across the
seas. They built many beautiful
temples and centres of learning.

After the Palas came the **Sena**
kings. The most famous among them
was **Lakshman Sena.** A great poet
called **Jayadeva** lived at his court.
Jayadeva wrote a poem called *Gita
Govinda*, which is about Radha and
Krishna.

Now you have an idea about how
India was divided into little
kingdoms more than a thousand years
ago. The kings were jealous and
suspicious of each other and fought
among themselves.

Mahmud of Ghazni

In the year A.D. 570 there was born in a little town called **Mecca** in Arabia, a great man. His name was **Muhammad.** He taught that there is only one God. God is all-powerful, all-wise and all-merciful. He also taught that the human soul can never die. There is life after death. We go either to heaven or to hell, depending on how well we live our lives. Many people became Muhammad's followers. They are called **Muslims** and their religion is **Islam**.

Before Muhammad, Arabia was full of warring tribes. His teachings helped reform their practices and unite them into one nation. The Arab tribes stopped waging wars against one another and united, they began conquering other lands. Very soon they had conquered Syria, Persia, Egypt and the whole of northern Africa.

The Arabs had been trading with India even before the birth of Muhammad. Later, many Muslim merchants came and settled down along the west coast of India. This coming was peaceful but the coming of the Muslims into north India was quite different.

Arab merchants had carried back

Mahmud of Ghazni

...tories of India's riches. In A.D. 712 a ...oung boy of 17, led an army into India. ...His name was **Muhammad Bin ...Qasim.** He marched into Sindh and ...tormed the city of Multan with giant ...atapults, stone slings and poisoned ...rrows. The king surrendered, and ...indh passed into the hands of the ...Arabs. The Arabs ruled Sindh for 300 ...ears, but could go no further because ...f the Rajaputana desert and the ...owerful Rajputs.

However, a time came, as you have ...lready read, when the many kings of

northern India started fighting among themselves. About this time a Muslim ruler called **Mahmud** ruled in **Ghazni** in Afghanistan. He knew of India's great wealth and his only desire was to loot India. Between A.D. 1000 and 1026 he raided India 17 times. On each occasion the Rajputs failed to stop him. His soldiers were good horsemen and fierce fighters. On every visit they destroyed temples and carried back treasures of gold and jewels.

One of Mahmud's worst raids was on the famous temple of **Somnath,** in Kathiawar. It was one of the holiest and richest temples in India. A thousand priests looked after the shrine. Mahmud marched 1,100 kilometres across the desert. Many of his soldiers perished on the way but he pushed on. For three days the Hindus fought desperately to defend the shrine but Mahmud's soldiers hacked their way into the temple and plundered everything. The priests begged them to spare the image of Shiva but they smashed it to pieces. The magnificent gates of the temple were taken out and carried off to Ghazni and set up in Mahmud's palace.

Most of the wealth taken away was used in building mosques and libraries in Ghazni. Mahmud thought that all that he had done was for the good of Islam. Although he was a plunderer, he enjoyed the company of poets and scholars. The two great writers, **Firdausi** and **Al Beruni** lived in his court.

Delhi Becomes the Capital

Muhammad of Ghor

The many Indian kings did not learn anything from the raids of Mahmud. They continued to fight among themselves, but fortunately for about 160 years after Mahmud, the country did not face any foreign invasion. Then, in A.D. 1191, another Turkish invader called **Muhammad of Ghor** attacked India. Prithviraj Chauhan, about whom you have read already, faced this attack.

The two armies met at **Tarain.** The Rajputs fought so well that Muhammad barely managed to escape with his life. He fled back to Afghanistan but could not forget the disaster. He vowed to avenge his defeat.

The following year he returned with a fine army of about 1,20,000 men. Prithviraj was ready to face him again but his father-in-law, Jayachandra, and the ruler of Gujarat both refused to help him. Jayachandra had not forgiven the hurt Prithviraj had caused him by forcibly taking away his daughter.

Encouraged by his courageous wife, Prithviraj met the invader on the same battlefield. This time Prithviraj was defeated and killed. His queen and her attendants committed *Jauhar.* Muhammad Ghori won the throne of Delhi. Jayachandra was not spared either. Muhammad defeated and killed him in a battle in the year 1194.

Muhammad's aim was not just to loot the country. He wanted to set up a kingdom in India. So when he returned, he left behind his general, **Qutbuddin Aibak,** to look after the lands he had conquered. Qutbuddin

74

did not sit idle. He conquered many more kingdoms for his master. Soon Bundelkhand and Gujarat were added to the kingdom. Muslim armies marched across Bihar and defeated the Sena kings of Bengal. Many Buddhist monasteries and centres of learning were destroyed. Some of the Buddhist monks fled to Tibet with whatever books they could carry. When Muhammad Ghori died in 1206, Qutbuddin became the Sultan of Delhi and for more than 600 years after him, all the kings on the throne of Delhi were Muslim.

Qutbuddin Aibak ruled for only four years. He is said to have destroyed 27 Hindu temples to collect material for his buildings. He began the construction of the famous **Qutab Minar. Iltutmish** who succeeded him was a capable ruler. He dealt cleverly with every danger he faced. By A.D. 1220 he was totally in command of his kingdom.

The sons of Iltutmish were quite worthless and so before his death in A.D. 1236 he had decided that his daughter, **Raziya,** should rule after him. Raziya was a wise and capable queen. She dressed like a man, and rode an elephant at the head of her troops. Raziya was the only Muslim queen to sit on the throne of Delhi. Many of her officers did not like

Qutab Minar

75

being ruled by a woman and so they plotted against her and had her killed in A.D. 1240.

The murder of the queen was followed by confusion and more murders. Finally, in A.D. 1248 the youngest son of Iltutmish, **Nasiruddin** was placed on the throne. He was a good person and spent most of his time in prayer. But he was quite unfit to be a ruler. All the official work was done by a clever man called **Balban.**

When Nasiruddin died in A.D. 1266, Balban became the ruler. He ruled with justice and with a firm hand. He kept a strong army and controlled the people through fear and force. But his descendants were weak and worthless. As a result, in A.D. 1290 the throne of Delhi passed into the hands of a Turkish family called the **Khiljis.**

The most famous king among the Khiljis was **Alauddin.** He came to the throne by killing his own uncle **Jalaluddin.** Alauddin was a brilliant general and a clever ruler. When he became king, he gave orders that there were to be no parties, no drinking and no gambling. He fought the Rajput kings and extended his empire in the south. He kept a large army. One of his generals, **Malik Kafur,** invaded the Tamil kingdoms in the south and returned with great riches, pearls and precious stones and over 3,556 tonnes of gold!

Alauddin was temperamental. He could be very cruel, but he could also be very just. It was reported to him that in the bazaars of Delhi shopkeepers were cheating people. Alauddin was so angry that he passed laws against the dishonest traders and appointed *darogas* or policemen to keep a watch. Alauddin could barely read or write, but at his court lived a great poet called **Amir Khushro.** He composed many poems and clever riddles. The modern *sitar* and the *tabla* are said to be his inventions.

Alauddin died in A.D. 1316,

Off to Daulatabad

probably murdered by his general, Malik Kafur. Kafur was himself murdered a month later. There was confusion in the kingdom till A.D. 1320. Then a new family, the Tuglaqs took control of the throne. Muhammad Tuglaq who ruled for about 25 years, was a strange man. He was brilliant and very learned but some of his ideas brought suffering and misery to his people.

Once he decided to transfer his capital from Delhi to far off **Devagiri** in the Deccan. The idea was to be at the centre of the kingdom and for this

he built a new road and arranged for free stay for people on the way. All men, women and children and even beggars were ordered to move to the new capital which he had renamed **Daulatabad**. The plan failed and two years later the capital had to be moved back to Delhi.

On another occasion he decided to have copper coins instead of gold and silver coins. The copper coins were stamped to show their value in gold or silver. But the minting of these coins was not properly controlled. Everyone began to make his own

77

Timur at Delhi

copper coins. Gold and silver disappeared and there were so many copper coins that they were worth nothing. The Sultan had to change his order.

While Muhammad was busy with his wild plans, his kingdom began to fall apart and various parts became independent. **Firoz Shah** who succeeded Tuglaq tried to repair the damage. He decided not to waste money on wars. Instead he built canals, bridges, tanks, colleges and hospitals. He was fond of learning and had many ancient Sanskrit books translated into Arabic.

What was left of the Tuglaq empire broke up soon. By the end of the fourteenth century only the Punjab and the areas around Delhi remained with them. The final blow was dealt by **Timur,** a fierce Mongol who came from **Samarkand** in Central Asia.

Timur had heard of the riches of Hindustan. One summer, he left Samarkand with an army of about 90,000 horsemen. It took him nearly six months to reach Delhi. So weak were the Tuglaq rulers now that he reached the outskirts of the capital practically unopposed. After a fierce battle he entered the city. For five days he looted and killed and then left for Samarkand with what he had gathered.

Timur left behind one of his officers named **Khizr Khan** who later proclaimed himself Sultan of Delhi. The **Sayyad** dynasty which he founded ruled Delhi for 37 years. It was followed by an Afghan dynasty, the **Lodhis.** But the kingdom which they ruled did not extend much beyond Delhi.

Living Together

The Muslims, who came to India, brought with them a new religion and a different way of life. They settled down and made India their home. They mixed with the Hindus and learnt some of their customs. Some of the Hindus were forcibly converted to Islam by the Sultans. Some others accepted **Islam** of their own free will. But despite the power of the Sultans and the attractions of a new religion, most of the Hindus did not change their religion.

When the Hindus and Muslims started living together interesting things happened. The language of the Muslims was **Arabic.** In the areas around Delhi most people spoke **Hindi.** The Persian and Arabic spoken by the Muslims gradually mixed with Hindi and a new language called **Urdu** was born. It had Hindi grammar and Persian and Arabic words.

Muslims brought with them new building styles and different methods of construction. Often Hindu craftsmen were employed and they used locally available material for the

Kathak

Sitar

Tabla

79

Pyjama and Kaftan

Salwar Kameez

Ghazal

buildings. So a mixed style of architecture called **Indo-Islamic** architecture developed in India. A new form of dance called **Kathak** emerged. In this the dancer wore Persian costumes but acted out Hindu stories. The *ghazal*, a form of Persian poetry, found its way into Urdu. **Amir Khushro,** the great poet, combined the Indian *veena* with the Persian *tanpura* to make a new instrument, the sitar. He also altered the south Indian drum to make the *tabla*.

Changes took place in the areas of dress, food and medicine. The *pyjama*, *kaftan* and *salwar kameez* as items of clothing, *biryani* and wine as items of food and *Yunani* medicine became popular with most people.

What kind of life did the ordinary people live? There was, indeed, a lot of difference between the rich and the poor people. The poor were not concerned about who ruled the country, for they believed that their condition would remain the same. Often, when great battles were being fought nearby, farmers were seen coolly doing their work in the fields. They hardly cared who won or who lost! The caste system had become more rigid and the lower castes felt the brunt of the bad treatment meted out to the poor and needy sections of society.

80

The Bhaktas

Mirabai

The coming of a new religion, however, helped strengthen the Hindu religion. Hindu rulers such as the Rajputs and the kings of Vijayanagar in the south not only resisted the Muslims but also became eager defenders of the Hindu faith.

On the other hand some ordinary people found a new way of looking at religion and God. It was the way of the **Bhaktas**. It started in Mysore led by **Basava** the founder of the **Virashaiva** sect, and soon spread across the whole country. It came to be known as the **Bhakti** movement. *Bhakti* simply means devotion or love. The saints who preached it are called *bhaktas*. The path of *bhakti* brought the Hindus and Muslims closer. It bound different parts of India in a common bond and gave new hope for the ordinary people.

Basava preached that all men are equal. He spoke fearlessly against social evils such as child marriage, ill treatment of widows, worship of idols, trees, animals and stones. He said that there is only one God. In Maharashtra, **Dyaneshwar** and **Namdev** spread the message of love through beautiful poems.

The bhakti movement also spread to north India. One of the famous *bhaktas* was a princess, called

81

Chaitanya

India. He held gatherings wherever he went and organized *sankirtans* or public singing in praise of God. The *Bhaktas* were not scholars who preached in temples. They were simple men and women who went from place to place singing hymns. They belonged to all classes, castes and occupations. They encouraged all people, even outcasts, to join them.

There were also other *Bhaktas* who were influenced by *Sufis*. *Sufis* were Muslim saints who had come to India with the Turkish invaders. They led a simple life and preached equality. They mixed freely with Hindu saints and gurus. Their ideas of God being present everywhere, and that he could be reached through meditation and love, were easily understood by the Indian people. **Ramananda** who lived in the fourteenth century was greatly influenced by the *Sufis*. He preached devotion to Rama. Among his close followers were not only an untouchable leather-worker and a barber but also a Muslim weaver named **Kabir.**

Mirabai. She was married into the royal family of Mewar, but fine clothes, precious jewels and all the comforts of the palace meant nothing to her. Her thoughts were only for Lord Krishna whom she loved. She composed beautiful songs in his honour and spent her time singing them.

Surdas, a blind poet from Agra, **Dadu** and **Narsi Mehta** from Gujarat, and **Chaitanya** a school teacher from Bengal, devoted their lives to spreading the message of *bhakti.* Chaitanya travelled widely in

Kabir was the son of a Brahmin widow. He was abandoned by his mother but rescued and brought up by a Muslim weaver. Kabir taught that God is one, whether we worship him as Allah or Rama. Fasting or telling of beads is of no use if we have no true devotion. God is not to be found in stone images and holy books. He only lives in a heart that is full of love.

Kabir

Among Kabir's disciples, there were both Hindus and Muslims. There is a legend that when he died, the Hindus wanted to burn his body while the Muslims wanted to bury it. There was a quarrel and when the sheet over his dead body was removed, there was just a heap of rose petals!

Another great saint, **Guru Nanak,** was born in 1469. Like Kabir, he taught that all men were equal in the eyes of God.

'God will not ask a man his tribe or sect, but what he has done,' he said.

Guru Nanak went on a pilgrimage to Muslim and Hindu holy places. He accepted many good things from both Hinduism and Islam. He preached against image worship, the caste system and meaningless religious practices. Once a Muslim scolded him for sleeping with his feet towards Mecca.

'Tell me a direction where God is not present so I can turn my feet there,' Guru Nanak replied.

Guru Nanak's followers came to be known as Sikhs.

The *Bhaktas* spoke and wrote the language of the ordinary people. They said that even the poorest of the poor could reach God without the help of priests and without religious ceremonies. All they need is a heart filled with love or devotion.

Many Kingdoms

The parts which broke off from the Sultanate of Delhi became independent kingdoms. These were Gujarat, Malwa, Jaunpur and Bengal. In south India three kingdoms became important. Two of these, **Warangal** and **Vijayanagar,** were ruled over by Hindu kings. The third, the **Bahmani** kingdom, established by an Afghan official of the Sultanate, was ruled by a Muslim called **Hasan Gangu.**

The capital of the Bahmani kings was **Gulbarga** and the greatest of their kings was **Sultan Firuz.** He ruled for 25 years and most of these years were spent in fighting his neighbours, the rulers of Vijayanagar. In all he fought three wars. He won the first two but was defeated in the third. After that defeat he gave up all plans of war and devoted his life to religion.

Firuz was succeeded by his brother **Ahmad Shah.** He launched a savage attack on the Vijayanagar territory to avenge his brother's defeat. He slaughtered twenty thousand men, women and children and forced the Hindu king to pay huge sums of money. He also conquered the Hindu kingdom of Warangal and moved his capital from Gulbarga to **Bidar.**

Krishnadeva Raya Receiving Visitors

The Bahmani kingdom reached the height of its glory during the rule of **Muhammad Shah.** He was only nine years old when he came to the throne. He was assisted by an honest minister called **Mahmud Gawan.** Mahmud was an extremely generous and learned person. He used most of his wealth in building a college at Bidar and providing scholarships to many poor students. He himself lived a simple life, sleeping on a mat and eating out of earthen vessels.

The firm control Mahmud had on the affairs of the kingdom was disliked by some of the governors. They plotted against him and tricked the king into executing him.

'The death of an old man is of little importance,' cried Mahmud as the executioner raised his sword, 'but to your Majesty it will mean the loss of your character and the ruin of your empire'.

He was killed but his words came true. By 1527 the vast Bahmani kingdom had broken up into five small kingdoms named Ahmadnagar, Bijapur, Berar, Bidar and Golkonda.

Vijayanagar, the City of Victory,

Krishnadeva Raya.

on the banks of the Tungabhadra river was founded in 1336 by two brothers named **Harihara** and **Bukka**. With the death of Mahmud Gawan in 1481 the Bahmanis became weak. During, this time an extremely capable king, **Krishnadeva Raya** came to power at Vijayanagar.

Krishnadeva Raya was a fine general and an able ruler. He often personally led his armies in battle. He was victorious everywhere. This was the time when the Portuguese traders had arrived in India and established themselves on the west coast. In the interest of foreign trade he kept good relations with them.

During his rule, Vijayanagar was at the height of its glory. It included the whole country south of river Krishna. Travellers came from Italy, Portugal, Persia, Samarkand and many other lands to admire the greatness of his rule. They were surprised at the magnificent temples and palaces, the well laid-out city and the fine horses and elephants.

Krishnadeva Raya, himself a great poet, encouraged other poets and also artists and scholars. The great Telugu poet **Peddana** lived at his court. Some of the best buildings of Vijayanagar were built by Krishnadeva Raya.

Krishnadeva Raya was able to keep perfect order and control over his kingdom. He also won the love and respect of his subjects. But after his death in 1529 trouble broke out in different parts of the country. The Muslim Sultans joined forces against one of his successors, **Rama Raya**. A fierce battle was fought at **Talikota** on the banks of the river Krishna. The forces of Vijayanagar were routed. The Muslims plundered the city for five months. Power passed into the hands of the Sultans but they too did not gain much from the great victory because soon they were fighting among themselves.

Babar

Babar

At the beginning of the sixteenth century, India, once again, looked like a patch-work of several kingdoms with their rulers fighting among themselves, which made India vulnerable to foreign attack. Babar saw this as a time ripe for an attack on India. He came to India to loot, like his ancestor Timur, but he liked the country and decided to make it his home.

Babar inherited a small kingdom called **Farghana** in Turkey from his father when he was just twelve. His mother's family was connected with the Mongols and so the dynasty founded by Babar came to be called *Mughal*, the Persian word for Mongol.

87

Babar Nama

When he grew older, Babar conquered Kabul. He felt that he should try and recover the lands that Timur had once conquered in India. He had been watching the camel caravans coming from India laden with spices and cloth.

He set out with only twelve thousand soldiers. In 1525 he captured Lahore, the capital of Punjab. After more preparations he marched towards Delhi. **Ibrahim Lodhi,** who then ruled over Delhi came with a huge army three times the size of Babar's. A great battle, now known as the **First Battle of Panipat,** took place in April 1526. Babar had excellent horsemen and guns. Guns were something new on the Indian battlefield. Ibrahim's elephants got frightened of the sound and turned back. In the confusion they trampled

upon the soldiers of their own side. The battle did not last long. By evening, the same day, Ibrahim and fifteen thousand of his men lay dead on the field. Babar was proclaimed Emperor of Delhi.

Babar's work in India had just begun. There was a brave Rajput, **Rana Sangha** of **Mewar**, who had longed to conquer Delhi. He was the hero of many a battle. He had already lost an eye and an arm in battle. Now he marched against Babar with a huge army. There was a fierce battle at **Khanua**, a village near Agra, in 1527. The Rajputs fought with valour but Babar's horsemen and guns won the day. Babar took control of the very heart of Hindustan.

Babar fought one more battle, two years later, and defeated the rebellious Afghan chiefs of Bihar. With this his empire now stretched from the Hindukush mountains to the borders of Bengal.

Babar was not only a great general but also a learned man. He wrote down whatever he saw and felt. His writings are called the *Babar Nama*. They are a valuable source of history. In his writings he had devoted about forty pages to India. In these he has spoken about its birds, flowers and trees, its houses and towns and of the good manners among people. On the whole, however, he found the country not as interesting as the home from which he set out on his conquests.

A King on the Run

Humayun's Tomb

Babar died in 1530, barely four years after he had taken Delhi. Humayun, his favourite son became king. He inherited a vast kingdom but it was not safe. It was surrounded by several hostile rulers. The most dangerous among them was **Bahadur Shah** of Gujarat. The first thing Humayun did was to march against him. He was just twenty-three years of age when he came to the throne in 1530, yet he was a brave and experienced commander. He captured the forts of **Mandu** and **Champaner,** scaling walls of the

latter himself with only a handful of men. Bahadur Shah was forced to flee the kingdom and take refuge with the Portuguese at **Diu.**

Humayun had one serious drawback. He liked to enjoy himself even when he had more pressing matters to attend to. Instead of making his empire strong and safe, he settled down to feasting and merry-making.

About this time, **Sher Shah Suri,** an Afghan chief of Bihar, rose in revolt against him. The fighting went on for two years. Humayun was

89

Humayun

finally defeated in 1540 at the battle of Kanauj. For the next fifteen years he was homeless. He moved from place to place for shelter. He spent three years in Sindh and Rajasthan. Here he married a fourteen year old girl, **Hamida.**

With a few faithful friends, Humayun crossed the desert of Rajasthan. In a small town called **Umarkot** in Sindh, Hamida gave birth to a baby boy they named **Akbar.** He was later to become the greatest of the Mughal emperors. Humayun had nothing with which to celebrate the happy event. He had a piece of musk which he broke and distributed among the few friends who were still with him.

Humayun tried to enter Afghanistan which was being ruled by his brother **Kamran** but Kamran refused him entry. After much suffering the royal family reached Persia where the Shah gave them refuge.

Sher Shah who took Humayun's place in Delhi ruled for only five years. He was a wise and able ruler. He was extremely active and took personal interest in the official work. He was very good to his people, especially the poor farmers. He built a network of roads. The longest road was the one that connected Dacca in Bengal to Lahore in Punjab through Agra. The road is now called the **Sher Shah Suri Marg** in his honour. Shady trees were planted along the roadside. Rest houses and wells were provided at many places. There were even post-houses and horses were used to carry mail to different parts of the country. Himself a devout Muslim, Sher Shah did not illtreat the followers of other faiths.

Sher Shah was killed by an explosion in 1545 while he was engaged in battle at **Kalinjar.** After him, his son **Islam Shah** ruled for nine years. About this time Humayun with the help of the Shah of Persia, recaptured Delhi and occupied the throne in 1555. Six months later, one morning, while hurrying down the library stairs, he fell down and was seriously hurt. He died soon after.

A King at Thirteen

The Gatway to the Jami Masjid
Fatehpur Sikri

When Humayun died in 1556, his son Akbar was 13 years old. His guardian **Bairam Khan,** proclaimed him Emperor of Hindustan. He was then in Punjab. Sher Shah's nephews Sikandar and Adil felt that they had as much right as Akbar to the throne of Delhi. Their army was led by an able Hindu general called **Himu.** He came marching along and occupied Delhi. Bairam Khan got together the Mughal forces and met Himu's army on the same battlefield of Panipat, where his grandfather, Babar, had defeated Ibrahim Lodhi. This battle, fought in November 1556 came to be known as the **Second Battle of Panipat.**

At first, it appeared that Himu would win but then suddenly he was hit in the eye by an arrow and fell unconscious. His men fled in panic and Himu was killed. Sikandar and Adil were soon defeated at Agra.

Bairam Khan managed the affairs of the kingdom for the next four years. Akbar was not interested in studies but spent his time in playing polo, hunting and riding fierce wild camels. In 1560, when he was 18, Akbar decided to take charge of the government. Bairam Khan was released from his duties.

Akbar believed that a ruler should be aggressive, otherwise his neighbours would rise in arms against him. He wanted to see his empire extended from Burma in the east to Persia in the west. He was indeed successful in his plan. When he began, his kingdom included only a part of the Punjab. By the time he died, he was the ruler of a vast empire that stretched from Afghanistan across the whole of northern India to the Bay of Bengal.

Akbar fought several battles and added a large territory to his kingdom. The Rajput rulers, however, refused to give up their independence. Akbar seized many of their forts.

One of the strongest forts was **Chittor.** It was built on a hill-top. Chittor was the capital of Mewar and was ruled by Rana Sanga's son **Udai Singh**. In 1567 Akbar marched against Chittor but capturing the fort was not as easy as he had thought. For four months his army tried to seize the fort but was time and again pushed back.

In command at Chittor was a valiant general called **Jaimal**. During one of the attacks Akbar saw him behind the battlements and fired a shot. The bullet found its mark and the brave Jaimal was killed. Udai Singh fled from the city and there was general panic in the fort. The Mughal troops rushed up the hill and entered the fort. The 8,000 Rajputs fought bravely till the last man. Thirty thousand people who lived in Chittor were slaughtered. All the wealth of the city was carried away to Agra.

Even after the fall of Chittor, Udai Singh did not surrender. He moved to **Girwar**, a valley surrounded by hills. Here on the banks of a lake, he built his new capital called **Udaipur.** His son, the

Akbar's Court

famous **Maharana Pratap,** carried on the struggle against the Mughals.

He fought the Mughal armies for 25 years from his hideouts in the hills and valleys. He and his band of brave Rajputs, slept in the open and ate the wild fruits of the forest. Finally, Maharana Pratap was defeated by the Mughals at the battle of **Haldighati** in 1576. He retreated to his fortress and held out there, bravely, till the end of his life.

By the time Akbar was 26 years old, he had many wives and a number of daughters but no son. In distress he visited a saint named **Salim Chisti** who promised him three sons. The promise came true and the eldest of his sons, **Salim** was born in 1569. In honour of the saint, Akbar built a new city called **Sikri** in 1571 and shifted his capital there.

Akbar was not just a great commander but also a very able ruler.

Birbal

Those Rajputs who were defeated in war were treated honourably and made viceroys of large provinces.

One of the things that greatly bothered Akbar was that people fought and killed in the name of religion. He believed that no religion could claim to contain the whole truth and that every religion had much good in it and so he was always eager to learn about other religions. He used to invite holy men of all faiths for religious discussions. He built the *Ibadat-Khana* or House of Worship for this purpose. He even started a new religion called *Din-i-Ilahi* or Divine Religion. He thought that this was a religion all people could follow. He hoped that this would end all fights that were fought in the name of religion. Unfortunately, he did not succeed.

Under Akbar, the people of India did not consider the Muslim rulers foreigners anymore. Akbar did not regard the lands he had conquered as an Islamic empire in which Hindus had no respect. People of all faiths were regarded as equal. The Mughals not only came to be accepted by the Indians but also respected and loved by people of all religions.

Akbar was convinced that he could not unite India into a single nation unless he won over the Rajputs and so he married the daughter of the Raja of Amber. She was the mother of **Jahangir,** the next Mughal emperor. Rajputs were appointed to high positions in his court.

It is said that Akbar could barely sign his name but he was always eager to learn. He was always surrounded by scholars, artists and experts. In his court were nine such men whom he called the nine gems. They included **Abul Fazl** the chief minister, **Faizi** the poet who translated the *Bhagavad Gita* into Persian, **Tansen** the great musician, and **Birbal** whose jokes entertained every one. Most of what we know about Akbar is from *Akbar Nama*, a book written by Abul Fazl.

Akbar's policies began to give the people of India a feeling of unity. They felt as though they were members of one large family.

A Scholar King

Jahangir

Akbar died in 1605. His only surviving son was **Salim** who was then 37 years old. He ascended the throne and took the title of *Jahangir* or Seizer of the World. He was an extremely gifted man and a very good writer. He did not change any of his father's policies but tried to improve upon them.

He is remembered for his sense of justice. He made sure that everyone, big or small, rich or poor got full justice. It is said that he had a big bell fixed near his room. A golden chain lowered from it hung at the gates of the royal palace. Anyone could pull this chain at any time of the day or night and bring complaints directly to the emperor.

In 1611, Jahangir married **Mehrunnisa,** the beautiful daughter of a Persian nobleman. He called her Nur Jahan, the Light of the World. Nur Jahan was not only beautiful but highly talented and educated. The emperor loved her so much that he did anything she wished. Her father and brother were soon given the highest posts in the government. Her brother's daughter **Mumtaz Mahal** was married to Jahangir's third son **Khurram**, who later ruled as Shah Jahan.

Jahangir asked Nur Jahan's advice in everything he did and many important decisions were taken by her. Jahangir was quite happy to let Nur Jahan run the government while he relaxed and enjoyed life. Soon her name appeared along with Jahangir's name on the coins and she became the real ruler. Fortunately,

Nur Jahan, her father and brother were capable persons and they governed successfully.

It was during Jahangir's reign that the British made their first attempts to send merchants and ships to India for trade. The Portuguese traders had already started business from many places on the west coast. Two British ambassadors, Captain Hawkins and Sir Thomas Roe came to India to meet the emperor. They were very respectful and brought several gifts to be presented to the emperor. They very politely requested him to let them begin their trade with India.

It is said that when they visited the court, Jahangir's daughter was very ill. Captain Hawkins who knew something of medicine offered to treat her and as luck would have it, the princess recovered. The emperor was happy and grateful.

'Name what you want,' he said to

Hawkins, 'and it shall be given to you'. 'I want nothing for myself, your Majesty,' replied the Captain, 'but help my country to trade with yours.'

Jahangir gave the British permission to start factories in certain cities such as Surat and Broach. He had no idea what this would finally lead to.

Jahangir loved nature. Ordinarily kind to animals, he once saw an elephant shivering at its bath and ordered that the water be heated. He had great skill in accurate observation and in writing. He was fascinated by anything rare and unusual and always wanted to know more about things and events. Jahangir treated people of all religions alike. He was friendly with the Rajputs. His kingdom was strong and prosperous. The arts, particularly, painting got special attention from him.

Jahangir's love of nature made him visit Kashmir many times. In 1627, while he was returning from one of his holidays in Kashmir, he fell ill and died. He was buried on the banks of the river Ravi.

The Emperor Who Built the Taj

The Taj Mahal

Shah Jahan who succeeded Jahangir was more adventurous than his father. He wanted to add more territories to his kingdom. He conquered Ahmadnagar in 1633. Three years later he went to the Deccan with a huge army. The frightened Sultan of Golkonda accepted defeat without a fight but the Sultan of Bijapur, further south, would not give in so easily. He fought bravely but finally had to accept defeat.

Shah Jahan did not have much success in the north. He lost Kandhar to the Persians. In 1645, he sent a large army into Central Asia but it had to come back without achieving anything.

Shah Jahan is better known all over the world as the builder of the **Taj Mahal**, the **Red Fort** and the **Jama Masjid** of Delhi. The Taj Mahal was built in memory of his wife, **Mumtaz Begum**, whom he loved very much. It took 20 years to build the Taj. Some of the best builders and artists of his age were employed and a great deal of money and time was spent. The Taj Mahal today is among the few wonders of the world. It is, indeed, one of the most beautiful buildings built by man.

Shah Jahan also ordered a splendid throne to be built for himself. Several

Mumtaz Mahal

Shah Jahan

artisans, and goldsmiths worked for seven years and produced a throne that cost over a crore rupees. It had two peacocks, blazing with precious stones of many colours. It became famous as *Takht-i-Taoos* or the Peacock Throne.

Shah Jahan and his courtiers lived in luxury. The palace was magnificently rich. Visitors from abroad came to see its great marble halls inlaid with precious gems and the wealth and the pomp of the court. The money, of course, had to come from the poor subjects, most of whom were just farmers. They were forced to pay taxes and grew poorer and poorer by the day.

When Shah Jahan became old and weak, his four sons began to fight for the crown. **Dara Shikoh**, the eldest son, was his favourite, but **Aurangzeb**, the third son was by far the most capable. He was known for his military skill. One day he defeated his brothers and imprisoned his ailing father in his own palace and crowned himself emperor. Shah Jahan remained a prisoner for eight years, until his death in 1666 at the age of 74. During all these years, the father and the son never met.

The Greatest Mughal

Some people consider **Aurangzeb** the greatest of the Mughals. He was an excellent commander and an able ruler. He was not only courageous but hardworking and is said to have seldom slept for more than two hours a day. Even at the age of 80 he continued to command his armies in person.

The first half of his rule was peaceful except for a few wars that broke out in the border areas. In spite of Aurangzeb's greatness and power, the people gradually became restless. Aurangzeb's officers found it difficult to control the people who refused to pay taxes.

In the northwest, Pathan tribesmen began to loot the caravans of merchants. The Mughal army had to fight several battles over a period of 12 years to bring the troublesome tribes under control.

There were also the Sikhs in the north, who were unhappy with the Mughals. Aurangzeb tried to force their guru, **Tegh Bahadur** to submit to his sovereignty. When he refused, Aurangzeb had him tortured and killed. The Sikhs were very hurt and angry. Guru Tegh Bahadur's son, Guru Gobind Singh, who was just a boy of 12 made up his mind to avenge the cruel murder of his

Aurangzeb Reading the Quran

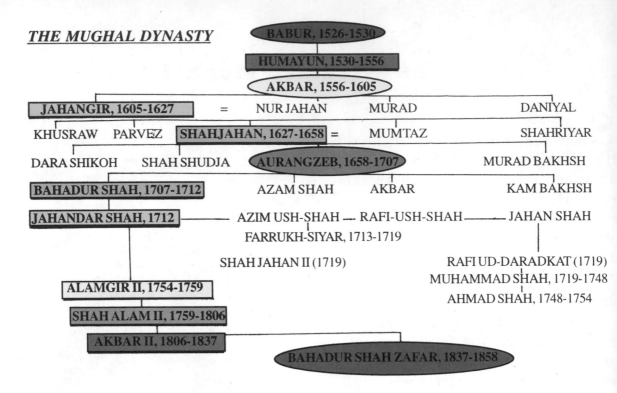

THE MUGHAL DYNASTY

BABUR, 1526-1530

HUMAYUN, 1530-1556

AKBAR, 1556-1605

JAHANGIR, 1605-1627 = NUR JAHAN   MURAD   DANIYAL

KHUSRAW   PARVEZ   SHAHJAHAN, 1627-1658 = MUMTAZ   SHAHRIYAR

DARA SHIKOH   SHAH SHUDJA   AURANGZEB, 1658-1707   MURAD BAKHSH

BAHADUR SHAH, 1707-1712   AZAM SHAH   AKBAR   KAM BAKHSH

JAHANDAR SHAH, 1712 —— AZIM USH-SHAH — RAFI-USH-SHAH ——— JAHAN SHAH
FARRUKH-SIYAR, 1713-1719

SHAH JAHAN II (1719)   RAFI UD-DARADKAT (1719)
                       MUHAMMAD SHAH, 1719-1748

ALAMGIR II, 1754-1759   AHMAD SHAH, 1748-1754

SHAH ALAM II, 1759-1806

AKBAR II, 1806-1837

BAHADUR SHAH ZAFAR, 1837-1858

father. He fought a long and bitter war against the Mughals.

Against the Rajputs, Aurangzeb gave up the path of kindness and friendship which Akbar had followed. Many of them wanted to be free of the Mughals. In 1678 when **Raja Jaswant Singh** of Marwar died, Aurangzeb tried to take over his kingdom.

He had Jaswant Singh's widow and young son brought to Delhi. This was to make sure that the young prince would never demand his father's kingdom when he grew up. But some brave and loyal followers of Jaswant stole into the palace one night and took the boy and his mother away. The Rajputs continued to fight bravely against the Mughals and in the end the emperor was

forced to allow them some degree of independence.

In 1681 Aurangzeb went to the Deccan and fought wars, first with the Muslim states of Bijapur and Golkonda, and then with the **Marathas**. At first, he met with success everywhere but the Marathas refused to be subdued. Aurangzeb spent almost 20 years trying to overpower them.

The Marathas lived in the hilly regions along the Western Ghats. They did not depend on any particular leader to lead them. There were several chiefs with their own bands of followers. They had a number of well-fortified forts. They kept harassing the Mughals from different sides. Their horsemen were skillful and used to a hard life. Since the

Mughal army was very large, the Marathas would refuse to be drawn into an open battle. Instead, they carried on what is now known as **guerilla warfare**. In small bands they would suddenly swoop down on the army, attack swiftly, throw everything into confusion and then retreat. The old emperor, who was now over 80, felt 'like an old bear plagued with bees.'

Finally, the great Mughal army was forced to retreat to Ahmadnagar. The wars in the Deccan had cost Aurangzeb a lot of money. Now very old, lonely and sad, the emperor died in March 1707, leaving behind a ruined Deccan.

Ever since his youth, Aurangzeb was a deeply religious person. He lived his life strictly according to the rules of Islam. He said prayers at the fixed hours and observed all the fasts. He lived a simple life. He did not drink wine. He banned music from his court and dismissed all poets, artists and scholars from his court. This was very different from the ways of the other Mughal rulers.

Unfortunately, he did not keep his religious views to himself. He believed that the only right way of living was by following Islam. As he wanted the whole country to accept Islam, he pulled down Hindu temples and imposed extra taxes on Hindu traders. He also reimposed the much hated *jiziya* on all those who were not Muslims. By these unfriendly policies, Aurangzeb lost the love and respect of the Hindus which Akbar had won for the Mughals.

A Rupee Coin of Jahangir

A Rupee Coin of Shah Jahan

A Rupee Coin of Aurangzeb

The Fall of the Empire

Nadir Shah

Aurangzeb's death was followed by a period of fighting and confusion. First, prince **Muazzam** ascended the throne and took the title of Bahadur Shah. He was already over 60 and died soon. **Jahandar Shah**, who succeeded him, was overthrown by **Farrukhsiyar** within a year. In 1719 Farrukhsiyar was imprisoned, blinded and then killed by two brothers, **Hussain Ali** and **Abdullah** with the help of the Marathas. **Muhammad Shah** was placed on the throne.

Muhammad Shah ruled for 30 years. And it was during his reign that the actual break-up of the empire took place. One by one various governors broke away as independent rulers. Muhammad Shah kept himself surrounded by musicians and dancers. He spent all his time drinking and feasting and came to be known as Muhammad Shah Rangila (or 'the colourful').

One of his nobles was **Nizam-ul-mulk**. He advised the emperor to be more like a real ruler but without much success. Finally, in 1724, Nizam-ul-mulk left Delhi in disgust and went south as governor of the Deccan. He later set up an independent kingdom in Hyderabad.

Plunder of Delhi

In the same year **Soadat Khan**, the governor of Oudh declared himself independent. Shortly afterwards **Alivardi Khan** the governor of Bengal followed his example. In the north, the **Rohilla Afghans** set up their own kingdom in Rohilkhand. The Rajputs too moved away as independent states. Soon the Mughal empire, which once stretched over almost the whole country, shrank to a few patches of land around Delhi.

Whatever little power the Mughal emperor had was further weakened by the invasion of the Persian ruler **Nadir Shah** in 1739. His armies marched practically unopposed through Punjab. At Karnal, barely a hundred miles from Delhi, the Mughal forces made a feeble attempt to stop them. The battle lasted just two hours. Twenty thousand Mughal soldiers were killed. Nadir Shah marched on to Delhi. Neither the Nizam of Hyderabad nor Soadat Khan of Oudh came forward to help the emperor. A few days later, some of Nadir Shah's soldier were murdered in the streets of the capital. Furious with rage, he gave orders to his army to kill anyone they wanted

103

Tulsidas

to, and loot whatever they liked. Thousands of men, women and children were massacred. Hundreds of beautiful buildings were set on fire. When he left two months later he took with him an enormous amount of treasure including horses, elephants, gold, jewels, the famous Peacock Throne and the world's most famous diamond, the *Koh-i-Noor*. The invasion of Nadir Shah was like a death-blow to the Mughal empire.

Rarely in the history of the world has a single family produced such a long line of talented rulers as the family of Babar. Most Mughal emperors were not only great conquerors and rulers but great lovers of the arts. Under them Indian painting, architecture and music reached glorious heights. The two great Persian poets, **Faiz** and **Ghalib** lived during Mughal times. **Tulsidas** who wrote *Ramcharit Manas*, and **Surdas** who wrote poems about Radha and Krishna also lived during the same time. Almost all the Mughal emperors were lovers of nature. They laid some of the most beautiful gardens in the cities of north India. The most famous of these is the beautiful **Shalimar Bagh** in Srinagar. Some of the most popular places of tourist interest today, such as the Taj Mahal, Red Fort and Fatehpur Sikri were built during the Mughal times.

SHIVAJI

Shivaji

During the reign of Aurangzeb, the whole of north and central India and a part of south India were under the Mughals. About this time there rose in the Deccan a brave Maratha leader, Shivaji.

Shivaji was born in the fortress of **Shivner** in the Western Ghats in 1627. His father **Shahji** was an officer in the army of the Sultan of Ahmadnagar. From the Sultan, Shahji received the *jagir* of Poona.

Since Shahji had to be away from home most of the time Shivaji was brought up by his mother, **Jijabai**. **Dadaji Kond Dev** was his guardian and tutor. Jijabai was not only very religious but also a courageous lady. She told him stories of the Ramayana and Mahabharatha and sang songs about the brave deeds of their heroes. Dadaji looked after Shivaji's education. He taught him to ride, shoot and to lead. His companions were tough and hardy shepherd boys of the hills. With them he rode the wildest horses and explored the thickest jungles. Soon he had a small band of loyal followers of his own. He now dreamt of uniting the Maratha people and seting up an independent kingdom.

When he was just about 19, with his small band of soldiers, he captured the small hill-fort called Torna, near Poona. He followed this up with capturing four more forts within a year. Unfortunately, by now he had spent all his money and had nothing left to pay his soldiers with.

One day, as he sat thinking in his fort, a messenger arrived.

'I have news for you, Sir,' he announced.

'What news?' mumbled Shivaji, fearing the worst.

'Good news, of course,' said the messenger. 'Some treasure is going to be taken from Kalyan to Bijapur.'

'We must get it,' said Shivaji becoming suddenly alert. 'There is a Muslim governor at Kalyan. He must be sending money to the Sultan of Bijapur. This is the money taken from the poor Maratha peasants. We must take it back.'

Plans were quickly drawn up and two days later, they attacked the treasure-train on a narrow, rocky road at the foot of some high hills. The attack was so sudden and fierce that the soldiers were quickly killed and the treasure carried off by Shivaji to his fort.

When the Sultan of Bijapur heard what had happened he was furious.

He arrested Shivaji's father, who was then in Bijipur, and refused to release him until Shivaji promised to behave himself. Shivaji was forced to stop his attacks on Bijapur territory for a few years.

During this time he did not sit idle. He brought under his control many Maratha chieftains who had grown powerful owing to the weakness of the ruler of Bijapur. By

Shivaji Meets Afzal Khan

106

He thought he could capture Shivaji through a wicked plot. He sent a Brahmin called **Krishnaji** to tell Shivaji that the two commanders should meet and settle things without fighting. Shivaji was not the one to be tricked. He managed to make Krishnaji confess that Afzal meant to kill him.

He agreed to meet Afzal alone. He put on a steel helmet and covered it carefully with his turban. He wore a suit of strong armour beneath his tunic. He hid a dagger up his sleeve and in the palm of his left hand he held the *bagnakh*, a row of sharp steel claws.

'I come as a friend,' said Afzal Khan as he moved towards Shivaji, 'I'm happy to see you'.

He saw that Shivaji carried no sword. He himself had his sword at his side. At first, it appeared that the two were embracing but actually Afzal Khan had held Shivaji's neck in a wrestler's grip with his left hand and struck him with his sword. Shivaji was saved by his steel suit. At the same time Shivaji had plunged the dagger into Afzal's back and torn open his belly, with the steel claws. A cannon was fired from Shivaji's fort and the Maratha soldiers who were hidinig in readiness fell upon Afzal's men and defeated them. The Sultan of Bijapur was forced to recognize Shivaji as the ruler of the whole of the Konkan region.

558 he had brought the whole of the orth Konkan area under his control.

The Sultan of Bijapur could bear no longer. He sent **Afzal Khan**, ne of his most feared generals, with large army to punish Shivaji.

'I will take the wretched Maratha risoner, without even dismounting om my horse,' he boasted publicly.

Shivaji Escapes

Aurangzeb, who had by then settled down as the emperor, sent his uncle, **Shaista Khan**, to crush Shivaji. The Mughal army captured Poona and Shivaji had to retreat to the hills. But soon he dressed up a few of his men to make them look like a wedding party and entered Poona. While the guards slept, he and his men crept into the kitchen, bored a hole into the wall and sprang into Shaista's bedroom! They killed his son and the Khan himself lost his thumb as he escaped by jumping through a window!

In 1664, Shivaji attacked Surat. The Mughal governor there was so frightened that he fled the city with his soldiers. The Maratha soldiers looted the city for four days and carried away gold, silver, pearls, diamonds and jewels.

Aurangzeb now decided to send one of his most powerful generals, **Jai Singh**, to humble Shivaji. Within three months Jai Singh had captured many of Shivaji's forts. Shivaji was forced to accept Aurangzeb as the emperor. He was asked to attend the Mughal court as were the other conquered rulers. Very reluctantly he agreed to attend the court at Agra. Aurangzeb always disliked Shivaji. At the court Shivaji was offered a seat with people much below his rank. Shivaji felt insulted and walked out of the court in a rage. Aurangzeb ordered him to be put under house arrest.

Shivaji was not the one to give up hope. Soon he began to make plans for his escape. Everyday he sent out huge baskets of sweetmeats as gifts to the Brahmins of Agra. One day, he hid his son and himself in two of the baskets and escaped from the city. Disguised as a *sanyasi* or a travelling monk, he returned to the Deccan. The joy of the Maratha

Ghorpad

people knew no bounds. Shivaji spent four years preparing himself for fresh conquests. By 1670 he was back at war with the Mughals, taking back forts he had once surrendered.

Shivaji used unique methods of warfare. He would never come out in the open because his army was small and ill-equipped in comparison with the Mughals. His horsemen would attack the Mughal army quite unexpectedly and then retreat suddenly before any action could be taken against them. By the time the Mughals recaptured a fort, Shivaji would be several kilometres away storming another fort. The slow moving Mughals could not keep pace with Shivaji's swift horsemen.

Shivaji used the *ghorpad*, a large hill lizard to climb the smooth and straight surfaces of the forts. A rope ladder would be tied around the ghorpad and the creature would dart up the steep wall of the fort. Then a Maratha would climb up the ladder and fix it to the wall so that the soldiers could climb.

The power of the Marathas grew steadily and in 1674 Shivaji was crowned King of the Marathas at Raigarh. His last and his greatest expedition was to the south. He conquered **Jinji, Vellore, Tanjore** and parts of **Mysore** in 18 months. When he died in 1680, at the age of 53, he was ruler of a large, powerful, independent state.

Shivaji was a great leader and a brave, fearless warrior. His soldiers and his people admired and loved him very much. People rallied round Shivaji because of his call to rise up in defence of their religion and their homeland against the Muslim 'foreigners'. He gave protection to Hindus but did not hate the Muslims. Shivaji possessed a lot of personal charm. Whenever he spoke, he seemed to smile. He had true concern for the well-being of his people and worked hard to improve their lot. He had all the land measured and fixed the land tax. He broke the power of the landlords who thrived on the toil of the poor. He commanded such love and respect that he moved about alone without much protection. The people of Maharashtra were always ready to risk all they had for him. Songs of Shivaji's bravery are sung even till this day. He remains one of the most popular heroes of our country.

The Marathas Won't Give Up

Shivaji's son **Shambhuji** was not a good ruler. He was never bothered about the welfare of the people and just believed in enjoying himself. In 1689 he was captured by a small party of Mughal soldiers while amusing himself at **Sangameshwar**. He was tortured and killed and his entire family, including his son **Shahu**, were taken prisoner.

The Marathas, however, were far from beaten. **Rajaram**, Shambhuji's brother took over the leadership. When Rajaram died in A.D. 1700 his widow **Tarabai** continued the struggle. For the next 18 years the Marathas kept harassing the Mughals.

Aurangzeb kept Shahu at the palace under his own care. He hoped to make him a Muslim and then send him back to his people. He, however, did not succeed in making him a Muslim but Shahu got used to the luxury of the Mughal court. Later when Bahadur Shah became the emperor, Shahu was sent back to Maharashtra. As expected, his return made the Marathas fight among themselves. Shahu's claims were strongly challenged by his aunt Tarabai. For a while, the Mughal trick seemed to succeed but gradually Shahu gained control of the Maratha kingdom and was proclaimed king in 1708.

Balaji Baji Rao

During his fight with Tarabai, a clever Brahmin called **Balaji Vishwanath** was of great help to Shahu. As a reward for his help Balaji was appointed **Peshwa**, or the

chief minister. In the years that followed, the Peshwa gradually became the most important official in the kingdom. After Balaji's death in 1720, his son **Baji Rao I** became the Peshwa. The post of the Peshwa thus became hereditary and soon the Peshwa became more important than the King himself.

Baji Rao was a brilliant military commander and a man of bold ideas. He immediately set about expanding the Maratha kingdom. By 1738 the Marathas had complete control over the whole of central India between the Narmada and the Chambal. After Shivaji, Baji Rao I was the greatest of the Maratha rulers. He had

Third Battle of Panipat

transformed the Maratha kingdom from a small state to a large empire.

Baji Rao's son, **Balaji Baji Rao** was just 18 years old when he took over from his father in 1740. Nine years later Shahu died and his son **Rajaram** became king. He was a very weak ruler. Within a year, in 1750, Balaji took full control of the kingdom and put Rajaram into prison.

In 1758 the Maratha armies went right upto Lahore, drove away the Afghan governor and occupied the city. But in the very next year they had to taste defeat at the hands of the Afghan ruler, **Ahmad Shah Abdali**, who recovered Punjab from the Marathas. To avenge this defeat Balaji Baji Rao assembled the largest and the most efficient Maratha army ever to take the field. They marched northwards and captured Delhi effortlessly. They met Abdali's army at Panipat. On 14 January 1761 in a fierce battle, the **Third Battle of Panipat**, the Maratha army was completely routed. They lost over 1,00,000 fighting men. This was a hard blow from which the Marathas could not recover completely. The Peshwa himself died of grief six months later.

The Maratha chieftains now began to quarrel among themselves. Soon the Maratha kingdom broke up into five independent states — Baroda, Indore, Gwalior, Nagpur and Poona.

Traders From Europe

Vasco da Gama Arrives

The Arabs had been trading with India for centuries, using the sea route across the Arabian Sea. From their own lands, they sent some of these traded items — spices, textiles, indigo (for blue dye), sugar, coffee and saltpetre (for gunpowder) — by the land route to Egypt. Here they sold them to Italian merchants who in turn sold them all over Europe. At each stage the traders made large profits and, therefore, the goods became very expensive.

The Europeans badly needed a sea route to India for cheaper trade. They also hoped to spread Christianity in the East. Many sailors set out but failed to find the route they were hoping to discover.

Finally, a Portuguese sailor named **Vasco da Gama** sailed round Africa and reached **Calicut** (Kozhikode) on India's west coast in 1498. A new sea route had been

Any ship sailing in these eastern waters without permission was attacked and its goods seized. The Portuguese thought that they now had full control over the Indian waters which to them meant anything from the waters off the coast of Africa to the Arabian Sea and the Bay of Bengal.

Now traders from Holland saw what the Portuguese had done and followed their example. Once in the Indian waters they challenged the Portuguese. There was much fighting between the two. The Dutch ships were faster and better designed. They managed to capture some of the Portuguese settlements. They established factories at **Cochin** and **Nagapattinam.**

discovered. Vasco da Gama stayed in India for six months and sailed back with ships full of spices and other rare goods. After this, Portuguese ships sailed regularly to India and returned to Europe with rich cargoes.

The profits earned by these trips made the Portuguese greedy. They decided to chase away the Arabs from the west coast and take over the trade for themselves. With their superior fleet they succeeded in taking away Goa, an important port, from the Sultan of Bijapur. They later turned it into the capital of the Portuguese empire in the East. No ship was now allowed to sail without the permission of the Portuguese.

After the Dutch, came the Danes, English and the French. The Danes established factories on the east coast at **Tranquebar** and **Serampore** in Bengal. The main settlements of the French were in **Pondicherry** in south India and in **Chandernagore** in Bengal.

In 1600 a small group of English merchants formed a company called the **East India Company**. They got their Queen's permission to trade with the countries of the East. Their first ships landed at **Surat** which was, in those days, a large port and a rich city.

In 1615, the English obtained permission from Jahangir, the Mughal emperor, to establish trading posts in several towns. In return, they promised to protect the merchant and pilgrim ships of the Mughals from the Portuguese. Surat became the main English settlement on the west coast. On the east coast they built a fortified factory called Fort St. George, near Madras. Up north, in Bengal a factory was built at Hoogly.

Bombay was then a small fishing village. It was given to the company by King Charles II of England in return for a payment, of £10 a year. The king himself had received Bombay from the Portuguese as part of the dowry when he married a Portuguese princess.

The English traders built forts round their settlements and began to keep soldiers and guns to protect themselves. Very soon their forts became strong and their armies more powerful than those of the Indian rulers in whose territories they were trading!

Most of the trade now passed into the hands of the English. The Portuguese and the Dutch were the main losers. The French, however, continued and set up trading centres. They too built forts at Pondicherry and other places. They were led by a very capable leader called **Dupleix.** He had dreams of building a French empire in India. On the other hand the English were led by an equally brilliant officer called **Robert Clive.** Both the English and the French tried to gain power by taking sides with the rulers in local quarrels. They even lent their soldiers whenever fighting broke out between two Indian rulers.

An English Settlement

Traders Want to Rule

By 1740, the Mughal emperor had power only over a small area around Delhi. His treasury was empty and his army toothless. In such a situation, there was a long struggle for the mastery of India and there were four main contenders – the Marathas, the Mysore rulers, the British and the French.

The rivalry between the British and the French was only a part of their wider struggle for trade and colonies. It led to some bitter wars between the two in India. Every time the Indian rulers fought among themselves they naturally arrived on the scene.

Chanda Sahib and **Muhammed Ali** were two powerful nobles. Both wanted the throne of **Arcot** in the south. Chanda Sahib approached the French for help and Muhammed Ali the British.

The French placed Chanda Sahib on the throne and sent an army to attack Muhammed Ali's fort at Trichinopoly. The British, led by Robert Clive did not have many soldiers. They knew they could not fight their way through to Muhammed Ali. Instead with just 300 Indian and 200 British troops they went to Arcot and captured it.

This forced the French to divert some of their troops back to Arcot. This divided their efforts. But Clive defended Arcot for fifty three days under most difficult conditions. Meanwhile, Muhammed Ali defeated

Robert Clive

the reduced French army at Trichinopoly. Chanda Sahib was captured and killed. Muhammed Ali was proclaimed Nawab. But, of course, he being only a puppet ruler, the British made him do exactly what they wanted.

In the north, **Siraj-ud-daulah**, the Nawab of Bengal was very upset by what the British had done in the south. He saw danger to his own throne and ordered the British to take down the guns from their fort at Calcutta. They refused to obey his orders and he decided to take action against them and marched on Calcutta. The British governor there was not an able man. Calcutta was captured without much difficulty. Now all sorts of rumours reached Madras about the treatment meted out to the English captives in Calcutta.

An army, under Robert Clive, was immediately sent from Madras to Calcutta. Calcutta was re-taken in the very next year. Siraj-ud-daulah was forced to return the trading rights of the British and to allow them to fortify their settlement.

Not satisfied with this, Clive now decided to overthrow the Nawab and establish a more friendly ruler. An elderly uncle of Siraj-ud-daulah called Mir Jaffar was chosen for the purpose. Mir Jaffar agreed that, if he became the ruler, he would make an agreement with the British and pay large sums of money to the East

India Company.

Siraj's forces were better equipped and greater in number (about 50,000). The British troops were ill-prepared and just about 3,000 in number. The two forces met on the field of **Plassey** in 1757. A large section of the Nawab's army was led by the traitor Mir Jaffar. It did not fight at all. By evening Siraj was routed and the next day Jaffar became the new Nawab of Bengal. He was, however, totally under the thumb of the British. He was a ruler only in name.

Clive first used his newfound strength to destroy the Company's European rivals. While the puppet Nawab looked on helplessly, the British began to help themselves to

Battle of Plassey

the riches of Bengal. Within days of the battle of Plassey, it is said that two hundred boxes filled with gold and jewels were sent to Calcutta as a part of Clive's share of the plunder! Gradually, the British also took over the *Diwani*, the right to collect revenue and administer civil justice in Bengal.

The king of England was very pleased with Clive for what he had achieved. He was given the title of Lord and was made the first governor of Bengal.

In the meantime, the battle of Panipat between the Afghan, Ahmad Shah Abdali and the Marathas had taken place. Though the British had nothing to do with the battle, it had

indirectly helped them. Ahmad Shah Abdali's presence in the north greatly weakened the Mughals' authority and the battle had shattered the Maratha army.

British rule brought misery to the people of Bengal. For several years the Company's officials systematically looted its wealth. The people who suffered most were the artisans, especially the weavers of cotton and silk. The British agents forced them to sell their produce at very low prices. If they refused they were imprisoned and flogged.

By the time Clive left India in 1767, the British, who had come as traders, had become rulers of a large and prosperous region in India.

The Tiger of Mysore

Hyder Ali with Young Tipu

When the British were growing in strength, an ambitious man called Hyder Ali, who was in the service of the prime minister of Mysore overthrew the Hindu king and ascended the throne of Mysore. Though illiterate, he had a sharp memory and he knew several languages. One of the British statesmen described him as, 'One of the greatest princes as well as one of the greatest warriors India has ever produced.'

With great skill he extended his power in southern India. In 1776, he invaded the independent kingdom of Malabar and threatened British trade on the west coast. The British fought an unsuccessful war with him and were forced to sign a treaty by which they agreed to help him if he was attacked by any other power.

Two years later when the Marathas invaded Mysore, the British did not help him. This turned Hyder into a bitter enemy of the British. In 1780 he captured Arcot and reached the gates of Madras. The panic-stricken British commander flung his guns into a lake and fled into the town. **Warren Hastings**, who was then governor general, sent a force from Bengal. Hyder Ali was defeated in several battles. In 1782, when the war was still on, he died leaving his son **Tipu** to continue the struggle.

Hyder Ali was a rather severe ruler but was able to keep his country prosperous and the people happy. He was extremely tolerant of all religions. When he died, Mysore was the strongest and the most united state in India.

With the death of Hyder Ali, the British thought that they had got rid of a very dangerous enemy. However, they soon realised that the new ruler of Mysore was even more dangerous. He continued to fight them all by himself. When the British saw what a fierce fighter he was, they decided to make peace with him. The two sides signed a treaty and the war came to an end.

Tipu spent the next few years strengthening his own kingdom. He was an able ruler. He introduced a number of reforms in the government and made new laws for the collection of taxes. He protected the peasants and even rewarded them for their service to the king. He tried to get rid of the moneylenders. The Englishmen who visited his kingdom praised the way he ruled. He was very popular among his subjects.

In 1789, Tipu attacked **Travancore**, a state to the south of Mysore. The Raja of Travancore was under the protection of the British by

a treaty. The British quickly came to the help of the Raja. **Lord Cornwallis** who was the governor-general himself took charge of the British forces. The Nizam of Hyderabad and the Marathas also joined in to destroy the power of Tipu. The war continued for two years and Tipu realised that he could no longer fight alone. He signed a treaty in 1792 and the war came to an end. Tipu had to give away half of his

Tipu Sultan

119

kingdom to the victorious armies. The British got control of the whole of the western coast of Mysore. The Marathas and the Nizam also got their share of the conquered territory in the north of Mysore.

Although Tipu lost a great deal of his kingdom he was not discouraged. In the next six years he was able to improve his military power and financial position. He got the French to train his soldiers. About this time Tipu also heard that Napoleon of France had invaded Egypt. He hoped that Napoleon's forces would soon reach India and crush the British. The British government in England also saw the possibility of Napoleon's forces invading India and sent a very able Englishman, **Lord Wellesley,** as the governor-general.

Wellesley wanted to crush Tipu before Napoleon's forces could become a danger to India. He sought the help of the Marathas and the Nizam of Hyderabad. The two old enemies gladly agreed to help the British. The gallant 'Tiger of Mysore' was left alone to face his three powerful enemies. The little help that the French in India gave him was of no use. Napoleon's plan of invading India failed. In 1799, the valiant Tipu died defending his capital, Seringapatnam.

With Tipu's death the British got rid of their most feared enemy. His family members were interned. Half of Tipu's kingdom was divided among the British, the Marathas and the Nizam, in which the British took most of the territory. The other half was given to the old Hindu ruling dynasty which Hyder Ali had displaced. The Hindu king was kept completely under the power of the British.

Tipu Sultan, the 'Tiger of Mysore' was more than just a valiant fighter. Unlike the other Indian rulers, he worked hard to make his kingdom a truly modern state. He brought experts from abroad to build ships and to make iron cannons, paper and glass. He imported silk worms from abroad and planted mulberry trees in several areas. This eventually made Mysore the leading silk producing region in India. His greatness, above all, lay in the fact that he alone, among the Indian rulers of his time refused to barter his freedom by entering into any agreement with the British. He lived and died for his dream of a strong and independent Mysore.

Tipu Fighting the British

The European Settlements in India (1705)

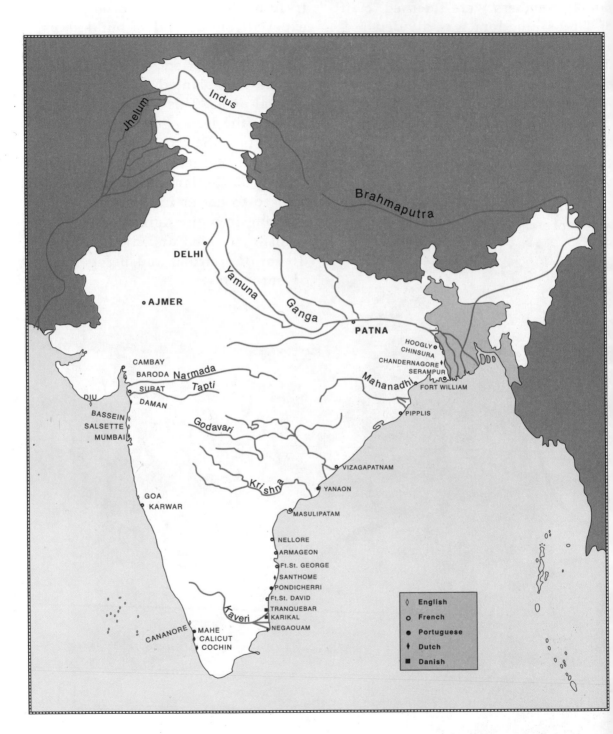

India in 1805

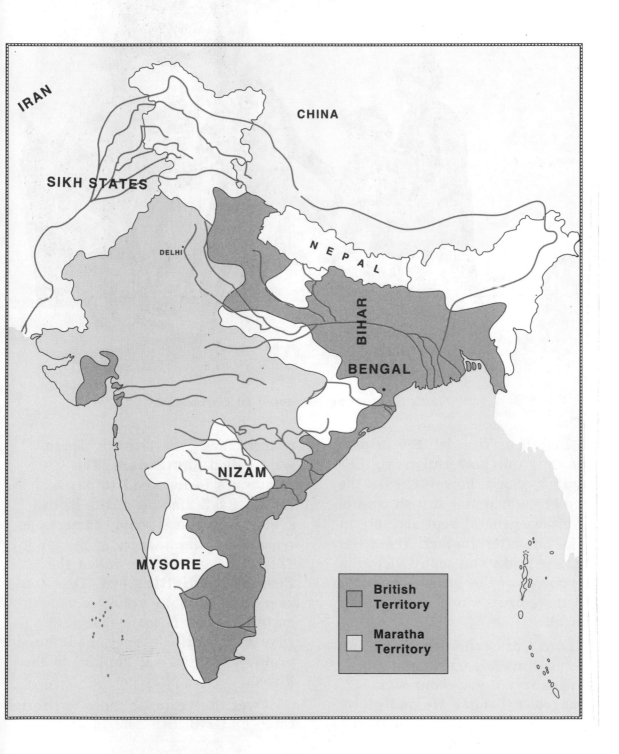

IRAN

CHINA

SIKH STATES

DELHI

NEPAL

BIHAR

BENGAL

NIZAM

MYSORE

British Territory

Maratha Territory

British Power Grows

Tipu's Sons Being Presented to Cornwallis

The fall of Tipu left the British with only one powerful rival, the Marathas. Soon, however, even they were brought under British control. Governors-general kept arriving in India, one after another. There were wars, setbacks and many victories. The power of the British grew. More and more areas came under their control.

Lord Cornwallis who came in 1786 had made some important changes in the way land was managed in Bengal. He had given some people the permanent right to collect taxes from farmers. These were called **zamindars**. The zamindars in turn had to pay a certain fixed amount to the British every year. These people came to be regarded as the owners of the land. This arrangement was called the **Permanent Settlement.** The zamindars actually collected much more from the farmers than they gave to the British. They made huge profits and remained faithful to the British.

Over the years, as more territories came under British control, the zamindari system spread to other parts of the country, especially Bihar and present day Uttar Pradesh. The result was that the poor farmers became poorer. They were not spared from paying heavy land taxes even in times of drought and famine.

Lord Wellesley's single aim was to make the British the strongest power in India. He achieved this in three ways: through **wars**, through a system called **subsidiary alliance** and by **peaceful take-overs.**

Under the subsidiary system, any Indian ruler who seemed threatened was encouraged to turn to the British for protection. The British promised to protect him and to do this, they placed British troops in his state. The ruler had to pay for the troops. If he couldn't pay in cash he had to give up his land. This meant that the rulers actually lost their freedom and became dependents of the British. Tipu Sultan was the only one who refused to accept this offer and for this he had to fight a war which took his life as well as his kingdom.

Lord Hastings, who became governor general in 1798, waged a war against the ancient kingdom of Nepal. From Kathmandu, their capital, the **Gurkhas** of Nepal had extended their power over the Kumaon, Garhwal and Simla hills. After three heavy defeats over two years the British forces finally defeated the Gurkhas and forced them to surrender Kumaon, Garhwal and Simla.

Hastings also fought the **Pindari** robber bands which terrorised people in the Deccan and in central India. They had their headquarters in

Hastings

Malwa. They would swoop down on the villages, looting, burning and killing. They had two famous leaders called **Karim** and **Chitu**. The British troops surrounded the area where the Pindaris operated and closed in on them. The Pindaris could not fight a regular battle for long and were soon defeated.

The Marathas were still in control of a few territories. In 1817, the British forced **Peshwa Baji Rao II** to sign an unjust treaty making him give up not only his claim over some districts but also the leadership of the Marathas. In response, the Peshwa attacked the British forces near Pune. The British were well-prepared. The Maratha forces were crushed. This was an important victory for the British.

William Bentinck, who followed Cornwallis was a governor-general who did a great deal for the people of India. He worked earnestly

Peshwa Baji Rao II

to put an end to some cruel practices among them. In some parts of India a Hindu widow was expected to burn herself on the funeral pyre of her husband. Encouraged by a few Indian leaders such as **Raja Ram Mohan Roy,** who had actually started a reform movement to fight this inhuman practice, Bentinck tried to stop this custom called Sati. He

Sati

Architecture (Gateway of India, Mumbai)

passed laws to punish people who had anything to do with the practice.

Before Bentinck, travellers were never safe on Indian roads. **Thugs** or robbers disguised as travellers would take innocent people unawares, strangle them and take away their valuables. Lord Bentinck tried to wipe out the thugs and make the important roads in the country safer.

Lord Dalhousie who came in 1848 believed in grabbing every opportunity of acquiring land and money. Within a year he fought a war with the Sikhs and annexed the Punjab. Then he fought a war in Burma to protect the interests of British merchants who had settled there. This resulted in the taking over of Rangoon and parts of southern Burma.

Now he turned his attention to the states ruled by Indian princes.

These rulers had already signed the treaty of protection with the British. Oudh was taken over because Dalhousie felt it was ruled badly by the Nawabs. Then he introduced a new policy called the **Doctrine of Lapse.**

It had been the practice of many

Dalhousie

127

The First Train

childless kings to adopt male heirs in order to ensure the continuity of their dynasties. According to the new policy, if a ruler died without leaving a child, his state would pass into the hands of the British. During Dalhousie's term, seven Indian rulers died without male heirs and the states of Satara, Baghat, Jaitpur, Sambalpur, Udaipur, Nagpur and Jhansi were added to the British domain. The treatment meted out to their leaders was a great blow to the pride and dignity of the Indian people.

Dalhousie also wanted to make India modern in the shortest possible time. He introduced the railways and the first railway line was inaugurated in 1853 between Bombay and Thane. Big cities were linked by telegraph. Stamps were used on letters instead of cash payments. A Public Works Department was set up to carry out important projects. Roads like the famous **Grand Trunk Road** between Calcutta and Peshwar were built. There were reforms in every field.

All these reforms were good but they were carried out rather too fast for a country not used to such changes. While a small group of educated Indians appreciated them, a large majority resented the changes because they went against their customs and hurt their feelings.

The Sikhs

About the time when Babar invaded India there lived in Punjab a holy man called Nanak. He was the first of the ten Sikh gurus and the founder of the Sikh religion. Even as a child he was so precocious and different from other children that the people said that they had never seen such a child. At school he learnt things so fast that the teacher thought he was a genius and would grow up to be a great man.

He grew up and got married but still spent most of his time thinking about God and saying prayers. He never even thought of food, a house, or clothing for himself and his family.

His worried family found him a job as a store keeper. Nanak did the job extremely well and his master was delighted but Nanak was not happy.

'What is the use of this work?' he asked. 'Why should I work for someone when I can easily work for God?'

Then one night he had a dream and he saw God himself standing before him.

'Forgive me, O Lord!' said Nanak 'I've done a great wrong'.

'What wrong have you done?' asked the Lord.

'I've thought, only of this world,' he said. 'I've worked for money.'

'My blessings are with you,' said

Guru Nanak

Guru Nanak and His Followers

the Lord. 'Go out into the world and help all men.'

The very next day, Nanak gave up his job. He gave away all his money and possessions. He kept just one piece of clothing to cover himself. He took a bowl so that he could beg for his food, a strong stick to help him on his journey and a mat on which he could sit and say his prayers.

He wandered from place to place. He visited many holy places and met many holy men. He did not like many customs and practices among both Hindus and Muslims.

'God is one and belongs to us all,' said. 'You will find him not only in your mosques and temples but also in your heart.'

Many people listened to him and became his followers. When his many travels ended, a wealthy follower gav him some land on the banks of the ri Ravi. There the village of **Kartarpur** was built. The Guru lived here till hi death in 1539. His followers came to known as **Sikhs.**

Guru Nanak's teachings are writte down in a book called the **Adi Gra**

fifth guru, **Arjun Dev**, turned the Sikhs into a warlike people. Guru Arjun Dev was imprisoned and killed for helping one of the rebellious princes. The murder of their guru caused anger among the Sikhs. They took up arms and resisted the Mughals.

During the reign of Aurangzeb, Tegh Bahadur was the Sikh Guru. Aurangzeb cared for no religion except his own. He arrested Guru Tegh Bahadur and ordered him to give up his faith. The Guru refused and was killed.

Guru Gobind, the son of Guru Tegh Bahadur, was the tenth and the last of the Sikh gurus. Under his leadership, the Sikhs became a powerful brotherhood of soldiers. They promised to keep themselves ready at all times to defend their faith and their people. They began to wear *kirpans* or swords. They were given new names with the title *Singh* added to them. 'Singh' means the lion. When Guru Gobind Singh died, he told his people that after him there would be no guru and they must accept the Adi Granth as their teacher. That is why the book is called **Guru Granth Sahib.**

From then on, it was a long struggle between the Sikhs and the Mughals. It lasted over a hundred years and cost the Sikhs thousands of lives, but they refused to give up their religion.

which is the Holy Book of the Sikhs. Before he died, Guru Nanak chose one of his faithful disciples to carry on his work and the tradition of Sikh gurus began.

At first, the Sikhs were a quiet and peaceful people, interested only in the worship of God. Emperor Akbar, who respected all religions, gave them a piece of land where there was also a tank. Here they built a temple which later came to be known as the **Golden Temple.** Around this temple grew a big city which we today know as **Amritsar.** It is the holiest place of pilgrimage for the Sikhs.

The Mughal emperor's ill-treatment of the Sikhs during the time of their

The Golden Temple

After Guru Gobind a brilliant Sadhu called **Banda** led the Sikhs. Battles continued till the Mughals sent a huge army from Delhi. After months of fighting and hardship the Sikhs were forced to surrender. Banda, his wife and their little son, together with thousands of soldiers were captured and taken to Delhi. There they were tortured and most of them were brutally killed.

Later, a daring young boy called **Ranjit Singh** united the Sikhs and turned them into a great people. He was short, frail and had only one eye. Yet he was a born fighter and an excellent horseman. At the age of 18 he became the ruler of Lahore.

Soon he added Amritsar, Multan, Peshawar and some places beyond it to his kingdom. He rebuilt the temple at Amritsar in marble and covered its domes with gold.

By this time, the British were the masters of the whole of India except the Punjab. Ranjit Singh was a wise man and he knew there was no point fighting the mighty British until he was strong enough to do so. He remained friendly and it was agreed that the river Sutlej would be the boundary between their territories. Ranjit Singh ruled for 40 years and worked hard to make the Sikhs a mighty power.

The period after Ranjit Singh was one of confusion and chaos. The British saw their opportunity and moved in their troops. There were four bitter battles. Finally, let down by some traitors in their ranks, the Sikhs were forced to surrender. The Sikh kingdom passed into the hands of the British. The famous *Koh-i-noor* diamond, which the Sikhs had won from the heirs of Nadir Shah, was taken away to England to adorn the British crown.

There was a sect of Sikhs known as the **Namdharis** or Kukas. They had at one time been soldiers in the army of Maharaja Ranjit Singh. On leaving the army they devoted their attention to religion, but still retained the martial way of life. One of their leaders, **Guru Ram Singh,** was a great patriot. He only used *swadeshi* products and had his own postal system. Under his leadership, the Namdharis boycotted the British educational institutions, courts, railways, posts and telegraphs.

The British watched their activities with concern and waited for an opportunity to crush them. In January 1872, when a party of Kukas was on its way to Amritsar to take a holy dip on the occasion of the *Magh Mela*, the Muslim ruler of Malerkotla, a puppet of the British, harassed them. The pilgrims remained quiet and passive for a while, but when the provocation became unbearable they made a

Ranjit Singh

furious charge and reached the palace gates of Malerkotla.

This is what the British had been waiting for. The deputy commissioner of Ludhiana rushed to the scene with a strong force and attacked the Kukas. The Kukas fought bravely but were powerless against a vastly superior force. Many were killed, 68 were taken prisoners. Of these, 50 were immediately blown up from the mouths of cannons!

Among those ordered to be blown up was a thirteen-year-old boy. The deputy commissioner's wife who was present on the scene was moved by the sight.

'He is just a child,' she said. 'He was perhaps misled. Let him go.'

'If he disowns Ram Singh,' replied her husband, 'I'll let him go.'

He summoned the boy. 'Young fellow', he said gruffly. 'The madam here, is sorry for you. If you declare that you are not a follower of that rascal Ram Singh, your life will be spared.'

When he heard his guru thus abused, the boy was furious. He broke his bonds and rushed up to the deputy commissioner.

'How dare you insult my guru!' he screamed, grabbing the Englishman's flowing beard. He held it so firmly, so the story goes, that the deputy commissioner could not free himself.

'Cut off this impertinent boy's hands,' he shouted beside himself with rage. The boy's hands were cut off. Then he was tied to the mouth of a cannon and blown apart. The young patriot's name was **Bishan Singh.**

Bishan Singh

134

Discontent Explodes into Revolt

Sepoy Mutiny

By the time Dalhousie's successor, **Lord Canning** arrived in 1856, there was unrest in all parts of the country and among all sections of the people.

People in general were disgusted with the unjust and greedy ways of the British. More and more wealth was going out of the country. Indians, even if better qualified and more efficient, were given only small jobs in offices while the British reserved for themselves all the important posts.

Indian artisans and weavers were unhappy because they had lost their livelihood. They found that suddenly nobody wanted their goods. The mills and factories in England produced cheaper goods and flooded the Indian markets with them. Indians were forced to buy these things. The zamindari system was making the lives of the poor farmers miserable.

The kings and princes had lost their power and were being treated shabbily by the British. Since they were not used to such treatment they were growing increasingly angry.

The Indian soldiers, who had so far helped the British to conquer India, were for several reasons not as

Attack on the Residency, Lucknow

dependable as before. They had many complaints. They were paid less than the British soldiers. They could not rise to higher ranks in the army. There was always the fear that they would be forced to break the rules of their religion if they were made to shave off their beards or give up their turbans or when they were sent to fight battles overseas. Whenever they protested they were brutally punished.

In Bengal, 30 soldiers had been blown from the mouths of artillery guns. Many were shot and hanged in other places. In 1857, a new rifle was introduced in the army. Its cartridges had a greased paper cover. The end of the cover had to be bitten off before the cartridge could be loaded into the rifle. The grease was made of mixed animal fat. This offended both the Hindu and the Muslim soldiers.

In Meerut 90 soldiers refused to use the cartridge. They were dismissed and put into prison. Then the rest of the soldiers revolted, killed their officers, released those that were imprisoned and marched to Delhi. In Delhi they declared the old and powerless Mughal emperor **Bahadur Shah**, the Emperor of

India and drove out the British from the city. Soon the revolt, known as the **Sepoy Mutiny** or the **First War of Indian Independence**, spread to Uttar Pradesh, Bihar and Madhya Pradesh. Some brave leaders led people against the British in different parts of north India.

It was very important for the British to get back Delhi because it was the centre of activity of the rebels. It had also been the capital for centuries. A month after it had been taken over by the sepoys the British forces marched against it. After a fierce battle lasting six days, they captured the city and the palace. The British soldiers ruthlessly killed hundreds of people with their bayonets.

Bahadur Shah Zafar and his two sons were taken prisoner. The sons were later shot dead, and the old emperor was sent away to Burma where he spent his last years in exile and misery.

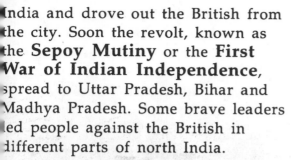

The revolt in Kanpur was led by **Nana Sahib,** the adopted son of the former Peshwa. Only about 300 British troops were stationed at Kanpur. The commander was an elderly man of 75. Fearing the worst, he moved his troops with their women and children into two large barracks. After resisting the attack for three weeks he finally, surrendered to Nana Sahib. When reports of fresh British troops marching towards Kanpur were received Nana Sahib ordered that all the prisoners be killed.

The next day, the British troops arrived and went after the rebels. Many were hanged and others were simply blown to pieces at the mouths of cannons. The British forces soon regained full control.

The same troops proceeded to Lucknow where **Begum Hazrat Mahal** had taken charge of the revolt. In Lucknow the British forces had been attacked from all sides and forced to take refuge in the Residency. The troops fought their way into Lucknow and through the streets to the Residency. But there they too were besieged. The British were able to free the Residency, finally, when fresh troops arrived from England.

Back at Kanpur the British were, once again, threatened. This time by another brave leader called **Tantia Tope**. Tantia Tope was a close friend of Nana Sahib. He had persuaded the rebels from Gwalior to join him. Taking advantage of the British forces being busy at Lucknow, he attacked Kanpur. Had he been a little quicker he could have even taken the town. Soon, however, the British forces returned from Lucknow and defeated Tantia in the battle that followed.

With success at Delhi, Kanpur and Lucknow the British had almost totally suppressed the revolt. But the struggle was far from over.

Bahadur Shah Zafar

The Brave Rani of Jhansi

Rani Laxmibai

The most daring and capable of the leaders of the rebellion was **Laxmibai,** the Rani of Jhansi.

In 1854, Lord Dalhousie had sent major Ellis to bring Jhansi under British rule. **Gangadhar Rao**, the Maharaja of Jhansi had died leaving behind a six-year old adopted son. Dalhousie had refused to accept the adopted son as the prince. Major Ellis appeared at the court and read out an announcement declaring that the East India Company would now rule them. The 17-year old Rani woud receive a pension and she would be allowed to live in the palace. Even as the announcement was being read out the Rani had shouted, *'Meri Jhansi nahin dungi'* (I'll never give up my Jhansi).

During the next three years Rani Laxmibai was forced to live quietly in the palace on the pension she received from the British. In June 1857 the soldiers at Jhansi rose in revolt. They captured the fort and killed the British officers.

In March 1858 the British attacked Jhansi. The Rani herself was in charge of defending the fort. As the soldiers fired the guns, the women worked at repairing the walls hit by enemy cannon balls. When the ammunition ran out in the fort, they hurtled stones and logs at the enemy below. At last, the British captured

Tantia Tope

the fort and killed the people inside.

However, the queen, dressed like a man slipped out of the fort during the night. She had with her a small band of soldiers and her adopted son. She rode all through the night covering a distance of 34 kms. In the morning the British horsemen caught up with her. While her soldiers engaged them in hand-to-hand fighting, the Rani escaped.

Meanwhile, after his defeat at Kanpur, Tantia Tope had decided to join Rani Laxmibai. But before he could reach Jhansi, his forces were defeated at **Betwa**. He now met the Rani at **Kalpi**. Their combined forces challenged the British but were defeated once again. With this defeat the rebels seemed to have been completely crushed.

Rani Laxmibai and Tantia Tope marched to Gwalior. There they won over the personal troops of **Sindhia**, the ruler of Gwalior, and seized the fortress. The British army rushed towards Gwalior, for the ruler there was their ally.

On their way to Gwalior on 17 June 1858 they faced Rani Laxmibai leading a small band of soldiers on horseback.

The Rani and her soldiers were all dressed alike in blue uniforms and white turbans. Close to the Rani rode **Mandarbai,** a Muslim girl, her close friend.

The British soldiers immediately joined battle. It was a hot day and

140

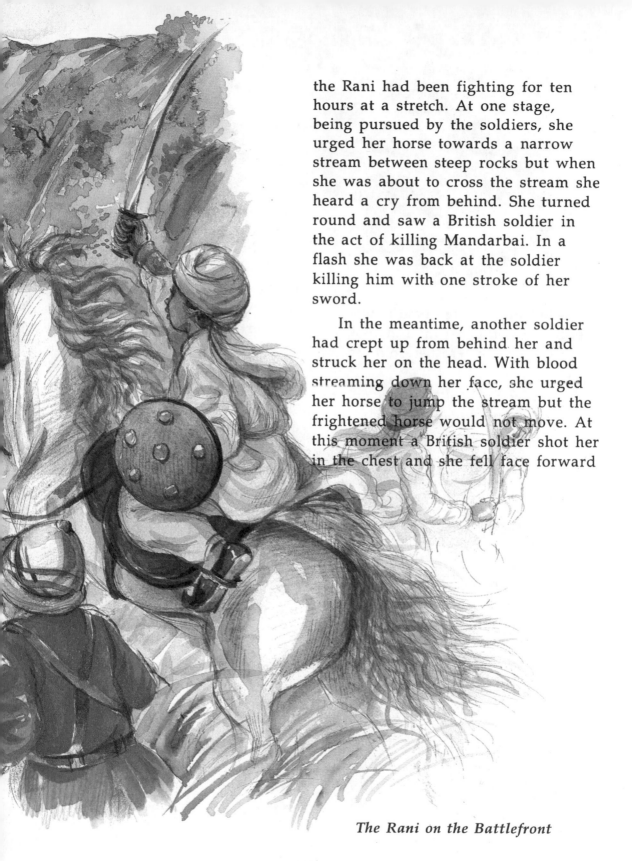

the Rani had been fighting for ten hours at a stretch. At one stage, being pursued by the soldiers, she urged her horse towards a narrow stream between steep rocks but when she was about to cross the stream she heard a cry from behind. She turned round and saw a British soldier in the act of killing Mandarbai. In a flash she was back at the soldier killing him with one stroke of her sword.

In the meantime, another soldier had crept up from behind her and struck her on the head. With blood streaming down her face, she urged her horse to jump the stream but the frightened horse would not move. At this moment a British soldier shot her in the chest and she fell face forward

The Rani on the Battlefront

Nana Sahib

across her horse. The horse now leaped across the stream and took her to the spot where her soldiers were.

'Don't let the British touch my dead body,' she whispered.

Her soldiers laid her on a haystack and as she breathed her last, set fire to it. When the British arrived they found only the ashes.

Tantia Tope escaped and carried on the struggle for a while. He was, finally, betrayed to the British by a companion and was hanged. On 8 July 1858, fourteen months after the outbreak at Meerut, the British had suppressed the Revolt.

The Revolt of 1857, though it began in the army, was more than a military uprising. It had the support of many different groups of people. Peasants and city-dwellers, Hindus and Muslims, soldiers and civilians came together in an effort to drive away the British from their country.

Unfortunately, the idea of a single, united Indian nation did not exist at that time. Though many Indians joined in the struggle, there were many more who remained loyal to the British. The south of the country remained aloof, and even in the north, Bengal and Punjab did not rise in revolt. Some Indian rulers such as Sindhia of Gwalior were on the side of the British and some rulers like **Jang Bahadur** of Nepal actively helped the British in crushing the rebels.

Though the rebels were sure that they had to drive the British out of India, they were not clear as to what they wished to set up afterwards. Many rulers had joined in the struggle only to get back their lost power and privileges. The revolt was not properly planned. It had no central leader to plan and lead the various attacks. The rebels were brave people capable of many heroic deeds but they lacked discipline. Moreover, the British were well armed and the rebels were not.

It was hardly surprising that the revolt failed but it was the biggest and, in fact, the only widespread rebellion against British rule. It became a symbol.

India Awakens

The Revolt had taken the British completely by surprise. For the first time they realised how angry and unhappy the people of India were with their rule. The Indians, too, had suddenly woken up. 'Why should a handful of foreigners rule over millions of Indians?' they asked themselves. 'Why should a tiny country like England control a vast subcontinent like India?'

The Western education which the British had introduced in India was having its impact. There was now a desire among Indians to think and act independently. By the 1880s no less than 478 newspapers, most of them in Indian languages, were being published. These did not just print news but began to criticise government policies. Many associations sprang up all over the country. A great period of reforms began. Indian people realised the need to give up their attitude of blind faith in ancient authority, tradition and customs.

Raja Ram Mohan Roy, Keshab Chandra Sen, Swami Dayanand Saraswati, Ishwar Chandra Vidyasagar, Annie Besant and Sir Syed Ahmed Khan were the leading reformers. Reforms touched all apects of life. Many social evils like Sati, female

Swami Vivekanand, Annie Besant
Sir Sayed Ahmad Khan

Dayanand Saraswati

what was actually going on in India. The British thought of themselves as superior to the Indians. They refused to be tried by Indian judges, had special carriages in trains, and did not allow Indians to mix with them as equals. 'It is one thing,' said Lord Lytton, the viceroy, 'to admit the public into your park, and quite another thing to admit them to your drawing room.'

This hurt the Indians deeply. At first, they were too weak and scared to speak out in protest but gradually the feeling of hurt helped to unite many educated Indians. They thought it was time to form an organization which would tell the British what Indians as a nation felt. As a result, an organization called the **Indian National Congress** was born in 1885.

infanticide which is the practice of killing girl-babies, and of not allowing widows to remarry, were discouraged. All the good aspects of our own culture were encouraged.

Traders and businessmen were now willing to set up mills and factories on modern lines. Indians began to run schools of their own. They began to hold public meetings and openly voiced their demands. They dared to draw the attention of the British to their problems and needs. Freedom from British rule was always the subject of their discussion.

The ideas of freedom and equality that the British taught in their schools were in great contrast to

Allan Octavian Hume

The Congress was supported in the beginning by a group of Englishmen. The most notable among them was **Allan Octavian Hume,** who is often called the Father of the Indian National Congress. A retired civil servant, he played a leading role in bringing the Congress into being. The first session of the Congress was attended by 72 delegates. Many of these later became important leaders of the freedom movement.

The Congress soon spread all over the country. It consisted of people from different communities, provinces and religions, the rich and the poor, the workers and the farmers, men and women, villagers and town dwellers. Soon the organization became the voice of the entire nation.

Surendranath Banerjee

Every year the Congress held its meeting in a different part of the country. At all these meetings there was always a strong demand that Indians be allowed to manage their own affairs. Till 1905, however, the leadership of the Congress remained in the hands of men who were moderate in their attitude and loyal to the British. Quite a few of these leaders were British themselves.

The most important leader of the Congress in its earliest days was **Dadabhai Naoroji**. He was highly respected because his thoughts were always for the country and not for himself. Through his books and

Dadabhai Naoroji

145

speeches he described how poor our country had become because of foreign rule. He was so truthful and kind that even the British regarded him as a friend. He demanded that Indians should be given more power. He declared, for the first time, that India's goal was *Swarajya* or Freedom.

Surendranath Banerjee, a great orator, pointed out in his lectures and writings, the need for national solidarity and the right of Indians to play an important role in managing their country.

Gopal Krishna Gokhale, who came from a poor family, had lost his father at an early age. He had often only one meal a day and studied by the light of street lamps. But he was intelligent and hardworking. He later became the Principal of college in Pune. He joined the Congress and founded the **Servants of India Society**. It consisted of people who pledged to keep the minimum required of their earnings for their needs and to give away the rest to needy people. According to Gandhiji, Gokhale had the gentleness of a lamb, the courage of a lion and was compassionate to a fault.

So far the national leaders had only used peaceful methods. But gradually they realised that the basic problems the country could not be solved by these means. More drastic measures were needed. Freedom could not be gained from begging, it had to earned through struggle.

Gopal Krishna Gokhale

Bal Gangadhar Tilak

Bal Gangadhar Tilak who lived and worked in the same city and at roughly the same time as Gokhale was impatient as a boy. When he was given a sum to do in class, he used to shout out the answer at once. This habit annoyed his teachers, but secretly they marvelled at his brilliance.

Bal Gangadhar Tilak tried to draw the common people and the youth of the country into the struggle for freedom. For this he used his newspaper *Kesari*. 'Freedom is my birthright,' he declared, 'and I will have it.' **Bipin Chandra Pal** and **Lala Lajpat Rai** played an important role in supporting the **revolution** as opposed to moderation and caution. A number of young people joined them.

Divide and Rule

Foreign Goods being Burnt

As the years passed, the Indian National Congress became a strong and truly national organization. People from all walks of life supported it in its call for freedom. The British began to panic. Several unpopular laws were passed to suppress the people's movements and activities.

Finally, the British used the Divide and Rule policy to weaken the freedom movement. They worked out a plan to set the Hindus against the Muslims. **Lord Curzon** decided to divide Bengal into two. The plan was to merge the eastern districts of Dacca, Rajshahi and Chittagong with Assam, forming a new province. The idea behind the move was to divide Hindus and Muslims so that one part would have mostly Hindus and the other part mostly Muslims. The reason given was that it would make it easier to manage. But the Indians knew that the British were being cunning. They just wanted to set Hindus against Muslims. It was clear to all that the partition of Bengal was to the advantage of the Muslims.

The Congress was quick to challenge the mischievous British move. By now two distinct wings had emerged in the Congress: the **Moderates** led by Dadabhai Naoroji and Gopal Krishna Gokhale, and the **Extremists** led by Lokamanya Tilak, Lajpat Rai and Bipin Chandra Pal. The two groups united to oppose the partition of Bengal.

There were more than 2000 public meetings to protest against the measure. The protests were accompanied by the **Swadeshi** and **Boycott** movements. People were urged to boycott British goods. **Krishna Kumar Mitra**, a popular leader of Bengal, said, 'Let us all, in the name of the motherland and for her good, take a pledge that whatever the inconvenience, when *swadeshi* goods are available, we shall never buy foreign goods.'

Rabindranath Tagore appealed to the people. 'The government is determined to divide us. But our hearts will never be severed. Let us tie *rakhis* on 16 October, (the day of partition) for rakhi is the symbol of unity.'

October 16, 1905 was observed as a day of mourning throughout Bengal. At the break of dawn, groups of people marched down the streets singing *Vande Mataram* a patriotic poem from **Bankim Chandra Chattopadhyaya's** novel *Ananda Math*. The poem glorifies the motherland and the singer pledges his love to her. People tied *rakhis* on every person they met. At many places there were bonfires of foreign cloth. Shops selling foreign goods were picketed.

Rabindranath Tagore

The British were besides themselves with rage. They warned the people of extreme measures. They banned the singing of *Vande Mataram*. These threats however, made no difference. The sky resounded with the strains of *Vande Mataram*. The British resorted to *lathis* and bullets but to no avail. The song of freedom was not to be silenced.

Soon, the washermen of Kalighat refused to wash foreign clothes, the cobblers of Faridpur would not mend English shoes, and all over Bengal English cloth, cigarettes and other goods were bought up and burnt in public.

'Swadeshi' and 'Boycott' had in fact changed the tone of the national movement. So far there were polite requests for reforms by well-mannered, educated Indian

Muhammad Ali Jinnah

The Boycott movement now included not only boycott of British goods but also of government schools and courts of law and renunciation of titles and government posts. Even young children were filled with the same spirit. Students refused to write on British paper.

The *Swadeshi* movement also created among Indians a liking towards Indian goods – an attitude which, in the long run, was to help the growth of India's own industry.

The Boycott movement was continued till 1908 but the government was finally able to stamp it out through more and more repressive measures. Many Indian leaders were arrested. Tilak himself was sentenced to six years' imprisonment. Three years later, however, the British reunited East and West Bengal.

Meanwhile, a new political organization had taken birth. This was the **Muslim League**, which had been established in 1906 by **Nawab Salimullah** of Dacca. The agitation against the partition of Bengal had been almost entirely Hindu and it aroused the fears of the Muslims. They felt they should set up a political organization to counteract the Congress. So the purpose of the Divide and Rule policy seemed to have been achieved.

educated Indian gentlemen. Now they were replaced by demands backed by the pressure of thousands of common people.

Meeting Force with Force

The Revolutionaries

Peaceful agitations, passive opposition and boycotts made no impression on the British rulers. Then what about meeting force with force? Wouldn't violent methods be more effective? This thinking became popular among the younger sections of freedom fighters.

Soon secret training centres sprang up all over Bengal. Here serious discussions were held and young people were trained in the use of fire arms. These young patriots were prepared to lay down their lives for India's freedom.

Newspapers played an important role in spreading patriotic ideas.

Writers such as Bipin Chandra Pal and **Aurobindo Ghosh** supported the revolutionary feelings. 'Nothing could be gained by begging and pleading,' said Aurobindo Ghosh. 'What we need is force.'

The youth of India were now determined 'to do or die.' They began to make bold attempts on the lives of British officials. Repression and injustice gave birth to terrorism. Killing of officers became an acceptable form of hitting back.

On 30 April 1908, two young boys, **Prafulla Chaki** and **Khudi Ram Bose,** fired at a British officer. He escaped injury, but two English women were killed. Prafulla committed suicide. Khudi Ram Bose was arrested and hanged. He was only fifteen years old. The entire nation was shocked at such a harsh punishment for one so young.

Lala Lajpat Rai was then the most popular leader in Punjab. Together with Tilak and Bipin Chandra Pal he played a prominent role in promoting revolution as opposed to caution and moderation. Many young men from Punjab joined him. But the British disapproved of his activities. They arrested him and sent him to jail at **Mandalay** in Myanmar.

This enraged the people of Punjab and soon slogans like 'Quit India, foreigners,' 'Go away, you double-faced, double-standard people,' resounded through the land.

Lala Lajpat Rai

Ganesh Damodar Savarkar was sentenced to life imprisonment for merely publishing a book of poems. Six months later the magistrate who had sentenced him was shot dead. An attempt was also made on the life of the Viceroy, Lord Minto.

Indian terrorist groups soon started operating in other countries too. In England, **Shyamji Krishna Verma** established the **Indian Home Rule** society. **Vinay Damodar Savarkar** took a keen interest in the work of the Society and secretly arranged to send arms to revolutionaries in India. **Madanlal Dhingra,** an associate of Savarkar, shot **William Curzon Wiley.** Dhingra was hanged and Savarkar was sent to India where he

Bipin Chandra Pal

152

was tried and sentenced to life imprisonment.

In America, the well-known revolutionary **Lala Hardayal** led the movement. All these revolutionaries were brave, self-sacrificing and patriotic young men and in their hearts even the British admired them.

In Bengal, **Kanailal,** a famous revolutionary was hanged. His relatives and friends went to take possession of his body. A British officer led them to the cell where the body lay. At the sight of it some of the visitors burst into tears.

'Why do you cry?' said the officer, comforting them. 'He died a martyr's death. The country that produced him is blessed. We must all die some day, but how many of us will die such a noble death?'

The Indians, by and large, were peace loving people and did not take to violence easily. The peasants and workers were untouched by the terrorist movement. Though, for a while, revolutionary activities outwardly appeared to weaken, they continued secretly behind the scenes.

One of the great revolutionaries to emerge later was **Chandrashekar** who took upon himself the title of *Azad.* When he was barely thirteen or fourteen, while taking part in a procession, he had shouted *Vande Mataram.* The police arrested him. He was brought before a magistrate. 'What is your name?' asked the magistrate.

'*Azad,*' he answered proudly, 'means free'.

He was stripped and flogged. Each time the lash came down on his

Azad

153

Azad   *Bhagat Singh*

bare back he winced with pain but shouted out *Vande Mataram!* At last he fell to the ground unconscious.

That first flogging really freed the boy. From that day, the severest hardships and torture had no effect on him. Azad, with the fearless **Bhagat Singh,** organised a countrywide revolution. Bhagat Singh had shot down **Saunders,** the police officer who had earlier beaten up Lala Lajpat Rai. One group led by **Ram Prasad Bismil** stole government money from a moving train at Kakori near Lucknow. Many of them were caught and charged.

Now, the revolutionaries decided to do something spectacular. On 8 April 1929, Bhagat Singh and **Batukeshwar Dutt** obtained passes to the visitors' gallery of the Central Assembly of the Parliament House. Once inside, they threw a bomb on the floor of the house. Later they fired shots in the air, and dropped revolutionary pamphlets into the hall. Then they gave themselves up to the police. The incident created a stir in the country. Large-scale arrests were made and trials were held. Several people were charged with 'waging war against the King.' Those imprisoned, went on hunger strike in protest against the way they were being treated in jail. The hunger strike lasted for about two months. One of the accused, **Jatinnath Das,** died after a fast lasting 63 days. The government finally accepted many of their demands.

The secret activities of the revolutionaries continued and many more youth, even within the Congress, were drawn towards the revolution.

Gandhiji Leads

In 1919 **Gandhiji** arrived on the scene. The situation in India underwent a tremendous change and the struggle for India's freedom took a new turn. He was just the person his countrymen had been looking for to lead them.

Mohandas Karamchand Gandhi was born in 1869 in the small princely state of **Porbandar**. His father was the *Diwan* (prime minister) to the ruler. Mohandas was a rather shy and timid child.

'I was a coward,' he said of himself. 'I used to be haunted by the fear of thieves, ghosts and serpents.'

He was even afraid of school and had few friends. He was a very ordinary child. Like most children, he went to school and just about managed to pass his examinations. At the age of thirteen he was married to **Kasturba**. When he was 19, he went to England to study law.

From his early childhood, Mohandas always tried to speak the truth. The story of Raja Harishchandra had made a great impression on him. He wanted to be truthful like Harishchandra all his life.

However, in his early teens he fell into bad company and began to eat meat secretly, smoked and stole

Gandhi — a Practising Attorney

Gandhi in South Africa

money. But soon he realized how sad his good parents would be if they came to know about these things.

At last, one day, he decided to tell everything to his father. He could not think of talking to his father himself, so he wrote out a letter confessing to all the misdeeds and promising never to repeat them.

The next day he went with the letter to his father's room. His father opened the letter and read it slowly. Then he closed his eyes and sat still, while tears rolled down his cheeks. He was sad and hurt but he did not show anger. Mohandas felt very sorry but he was also grateful to his father for not scolding him. The incident taught Gandhi the value of truth.

In England at first Mohandas tried his best to live like an Englishman. He wore a top hat, and took dancing and violin lessons. But soon he realized that this kind of life was not for him. He went back to a life-style in keeping with his culture and traditions.

On his return to India, he tried to practise law both in Bombay and in Rajkot, but was a complete failure. Appearing in his first court case, he was so nervous that he was unable to speak at all!

In 1893, when he was only 24, Mohandas went to South Africa in connection with a legal case. What shocked him there was the way the Africans and Indians were treated by the white settlers. They were not allowed to walk on the same pavements as the white people, or travel in the same coaches. If they did, they were insulted, tried and even jailed. Gandhi himself was subjected to such treatment.

Gandhi decided to stay on in South Africa. For the next 22 years he devoted himself to improving the humiliating conditions under which Indians lived there. He showed the people a new way of fighting injustice.

Gandhi believed that there is always a peaceful way of doing things. If one had to fight and hurt people to get something, that thing was not worth having at all. If he thought a law was unfair, he believed it was not wrong for him to break it and accept cheerfully any punishment given to him.

This way of fighting, without violence for what one believed to be right, he called *Satyagraha*. Satyagraha means the force of truth. To Gandhi, *satya* or truth and *ahimsa* or non-violence were the most important things in life. 'If I'm a follower of Ahimsa, I must love my enemy,' he said.

In 1915 Gandhi returned to India. First, he went on a tour of the country to see, for himself, the condition of the people. He saw that most people in India were poor and were being illtreated under the British rule. In addition to this, there were many social evils. There were practices like untouchability because of the caste system. The condition of women and the low caste people was miserable. There was disunity among the people.

Gandhiji decided that unity would be the most powerful weapon against the British Raj. He was determined that all social evils would be uprooted along with foreign rule. He also pleaded for a common language throughout the entire country.

Gandhiji Meeting People

The **First World War** had broken out with Britain, France, Russia and some other countries on one side and Germany on the other. Britain wanted help from India and promised that Indians would get more rights when the war was over. Over a million Indians volunteered to fight in the Indian army on behalf of Britain. The war dragged on and showed no signs of ending.

There were food shortages and rising prices. The government spoke of the need for loyalty and sacrifice, but said nothing of reforms. They said they were fighting to make the world safe for self-rule for all nations.

When, finally, peace came in 1919, the British introduced some new measures. These reforms were so half-hearted that it became clear that they had no desire to give Indians the power to rule themselves. There

was great resentment throughout the country.

Gandhiji, first requested the government not to introduce these reforms. On being ignored, he started his silent protest movement. He called on the people of India to break the new laws. There were demonstrations, strikes and processions to demand self-rule. The police broke up meetings. Many people were hurt and thousands were arrested.

The most serious disturbances took place in Punjab. On 13 April 1919, at a place called **Jallianwala Bagh,** about 20,000 men, women and children had gathered to hear their leaders. **General Dyer**, who had earlier declared all public meetings illegal, decided to teach the Indians a lesson. He proceeded to the place with about 150 fully armed soldiers. He blocked the only exit and without

The Jallianwala Bagh Massacre

158

warning ordered his men to open fire on the unarmed crowd. Since Jallianwala Bagh was surrounded on all sides by high walls, there was no way people could escape. Guns blazed away as people ran helter-skelter. The firing stopped only when there was no ammunition left.

Three hundred and seventy nine people were killed and over 1,200 were wounded. The British praised General Dyer for his honest discharge of duties! Gandhiji was horrified by the brutality of the British and the whole nation was shocked.

'Co-operation in any shape or form with this satanic government is sinful,' Gandhiji declared. His answer to the Jallianwala incident was *satyagraha*. 'A *satyagrahi* must not fear the oppressor, must always stand up firmly for his rights; and must not hit back when struck.'

This was the start of the non-cooperation movement. People declared that they would not co-operate with the government and would deliberately break laws.

Thousands of students left their schools and colleges. Many lawyers gave up practising law. Women and children went around collecting foreign cloth and made bonfires of it in the streets. People began wearing thick, rough khadi, thus doing away with the difference between the rich and the poor.

Gandhiji desired that the people's

movement should be non-violent and peaceful. But sometimes people could not hold themselves back. There were several minor outbreaks of violence. Then, finally there was a horrifying incident at **Chauri Chaura** in the district of Gorakhpur. An excited crowd set fire to a police station and burnt 22 policemen alive.

Gandhiji was greatly pained and decided to call off the non-cooperation movement. To him, winning freedom was not the only important thing, the means of getting it was as important. There was no place for any violence in his method.

Muslims had, from the very beginning, accepted Gandhiji's leadership. There was a special reason for it. During the First World War, Turkey which fought as an ally of Germany, had been defeated. In the Peace Treaty that followed, the Turkish empire was divided and the Sultan deprived of much of his authority. To the Muslims in India, for whom the Sultan was the Caliph (supreme religion leader), this was an unpleasant shock, more so because, during the war, in order to get the support of the Indian Muslims, the British had promised that the powers of the Caliph would not be reduced.

Indian Muslims, therefore, started what is known as the Khilafat Movement in support of the Caliph. Gandhiji saw in it an opportunity to unite Hindus and Muslims. He gave his full support to the Khilafat movement. A feeling of brotherhood brought Hindus and Muslims together. All differences were forgotten. Muslims invited Hindu leaders to address meetings inside their mosques.

It was about this time that another important person was drawn into the freedom struggle.

Jawaharlal Nehru had been brought up in Allahabad in the manner of rich British boys. He was educated, first, by special tutors at home; then sent to England to the famous English Public School at Harrow and later to specialize in law. After his return to India, he stayed aloof from what was happening in the country. Then, however, Gandhiji's new programme had a great influence on the young man.

Jawaharlal's father was a successful and rich lawyer. He was at first worried at the thought of Jawaharlal joining a movement that

Chauri Chaura

might involve his son being imprisoned. One day, he even tried to sleep on the floor to experience what it would be like in prison. Gradually,

however, he was convinced by Gandhiji's arguments and joined the freedom struggle himself. He gave up his flourishing practice, sold his horses and carriages, dispensed with his servants and took to wearing khadi.

In 1926, the British decided to appoint a commission to report on the possibility of a change in the Constitution. Sir John Simon was its chairman. No Indian was on the commission and this greatly angered the Indian leaders. So when the Commission arrived in India in February 1928, it was boycotted. It was greeted with black flags and cries of 'Simon, go back.' The most active among the opponents were students and young people.

While, in general, the **Independence Movement** was gaining strength something unfortunate was happening in the country. Relations between the Hindus and Muslims were gradually growing worse. In 1924, the Turks themselves abolished the position of the Caliph. This put an end to the Khilafat movement and ended Hindu-Muslim unity. Hindu-Muslim riots became a regular feature of Indian life. The British widened the rift between the two communities by suggesting that *Swarajya* for India would mean Hindu Raj in which the Muslims would be dominated by the Hindus who were in the majority. Many Muslim leaders like **Mohammad Ali Jinnah, Maulana Mohammad Ali** and **Maulana Shaukat Ali** left the Congress.

Complete Independence!

The 1929 Calcutta session of the Indian National Congress ended with the leaders determined to do all they could to achieve complete Independence. Accordingly, in December of the same year, the Congress met in Lahore. Young Jawaharlal was elected president. At this session, the Congress decided that it would not rest until it had obtained *poorna swaraj* or complete Independence.

26 January 1930 was chosen as Independence Day. On that day, in every town and city, people took a pledge that they would work for Independence. The Congress entrusted Gandhiji with the task of leading a **Civil Disobedience Campaign** against the British.

Gandhiji decided to start his campaign by breaking the unjust **Salt Laws**. Those who were looking forward to something sensational or dramatic were disappointed. 'What does he hope to achieve by just breaking these laws?' they asked.

Gandhiji wanted to draw the attention of the people to the fact that millions of Indians could not even afford salt to eat with their food. Salt was freely available along the long Indian coastline, but the British had made the collection of

Gandhiji at his Spinning Wheel

salt an offence so that they could sell the salt that came from England.

Gandhiji decided to walk to the sea coast and break the salt laws by collecting or making salt. For this purpose, he chose a place called **Dandi** in Surat district. Starting on 12 March 1930, with his followers from his ashram at **Sabarmati**, he walked for over 25 days covering nearly 300 kilometres. Arriving at **Dandi,** Gandhiji collected some water from the sea. He heated it and made five grams of salt. The salt was then auctioned in public and a businessman from Ahmedabad bought it for Rs. 525. The Salt Law was broken. Thousands of men and women, all over the country, now began to make salt and sell it in the streets in open defiance of the law.

Gandhiji next announced that he and his followers would raid the government salt godown at **Dharasana**. But before they could do that Gandhiji was arrested. Leaders like **Abbas Tyabji** and then **Sarojini Naidu** carried on the Salt Satyagraha. For weeks, groups of *satyagrahis* continued to make attempts to raid the godown. Mounted police charged them and lathi blows were rained on their heads. Many *satyagrahis* were seriously injured. Wounded and bleeding they were herded into jail.

The breaking of the Salt law was only one aspect of the widespread Civil Disobedience Movement. Soon it spread to other fields. Government officials resigned from their jobs, hundreds of village headmen left

their posts. For the first time women came out of their homes in large numbers to join the movement. As usual young people were filled with enthusiasm and patriotic fervour. Foreign cloth and liquor shops were picketed and every unjust law was broken.

The British tried to crush the movement. Many people were killed

Lathi charge at Dharasana

and jails overflowed with prisoners. In the northwest, the movement was led by **Abdul Ghaffar Khan**, in the northeast by **Rani Gaidinliu** of Nagaland and in the south by **Chakravarti Rajagopalachari.**

The British faced with a country-wide agitation, became anxious and the viceroy, **Lord Irwin,** released all prominent leaders and began talks for a settlement. Gandhiji had a series of talks with the viceroy and a pact was signed. The Congress agreed to suspend the movement and to send Gandhiji to attend a **Round Table Conference** in London. People were allowed to collect salt from the sea coast.

Gandhiji attended the Round Table Conference but it was a total failure. Gandhiji returned to India determined to renew his movement. The British arrested Gandhiji and declared the Congress an illegal organization. The government soon announced what was called the **Communal Award.** According to this Award, the untouchables were to be treated as a separate group from the higher caste Hindus. They were to have the same right to elect their own representatives as the Muslims had. Three different lists of voters would be prepared for higher caste Hindus, for untouchables and for Muslims. The policy of 'Divide and Rule' having separated Muslims from Hindus would now divide the Hindus

into two groups.

Gandhiji, who learnt of this announcement in jail, began a fast unto death. He felt that if the untoucables were treated as a separate group, this would only make their position worse. **Dr. B. R. Ambedkar** the Scheduled Caste leader did not agree with Gandhiji's idea that the position of the Scheduled Castes could be improved by getting the caste Hindus to change their attitudes. He wanted to get them political concessions so that they would be in a stronger position to demand their rights.

Fortunately, Dr. Ambedkar finally accepted Gandhiji's view. But the fast helped clear the differences between the leaders of caste Hindus and the Scheduled Castes. Under the leadership of Gandhiji, the caste Hindus later began a campaign for the removal of untouchability. The government modified their decision and Gandhiji called off the fast. He gave a new name to the untouchables and called them *Harijans*, that is 'the people of God.' He converted his Sabarmati ashram into an ashram for the workers in the Harijan movement.

Elections to the provincial councils were held in 1937. The Congress took part in the elections and won a majority in seven out of eleven provinces. The result of the elections was, however, not acceptable to the Muslims. It increased the gulf between the Congress and the Muslim League. Mohammad Ali Jinnah, the leader of the Muslim League, started a campaign against the Congress ministries.

Round Table Conference

Dr. Ambedkar

The Congress ministers on their part did excellent work in the provinces. During this time **World War II** broke out and without consulting the elected representatives of the people the British forced India into the war. This was an insult to the Indian people. The Congress ministries in the provinces resigned in protest.

In the meantime the Muslim League, under Jinnah, declared that Muslims were a separate people and, therefore, must have a separate homeland called **Pakistan**. All hopes of uniting the Hindus and Muslims in an undivided India perished.

Japan had joined the war on the side of Germany. In 1942, as Japan threatened to attack India from the east, Gandhiji once again gave a call for a countrywide Satyagraha. He asked the British to quit India. 'India will look after its own defence,' he said. 'If Japan attacks India, it is because the British had made India one of their military strongholds.' Gandhiji and many other important leaders were arrested. Gandhiji's call to the people was to 'Do or Die.' It meant either we win freedom or die for it.

The **Quit India Movement** spread all over the country. The struggle between the people and the Government had intensified. In the absence of their leaders, students, workers, farmers, men and women,

Gandhiji with Sarojini Naidu

boys and girls, took the movement into their own hands and began destroying post offices, railways and police stations. The police tried to repress them through bullets and arrests.

Meanwhile, one more great patriot, **Subhas Chandra Bose**, who had always believed that the only way to drive the British out was the use of force, felt that India must take full advantage of the war. In 1943, he took over the leadership of the Indian Independence Movement in Southeast Asia. He expanded and reorganised the *Azad Hind Fauj* or **Indian National Army (INA)** which had already been formed with the help of Indian prisoners-of-war who had fallen into Japanese hands.

At a meeting in Singapore, Bose took an oath to liberate India and his countrymen. Troops from the INA advanced with the Japanese army to the very borders of India. They crossed the Burma-India border in 1944 and

Subhash Chandra Bose and INA

triumphantly planted the Indian flag at Moirang in Manipur in April. But then disaster struck. Torrential rains came down, communications were cut, and cholera and malaria swept through the army. The Japanese began losing ground on India's eastern frontier. They were also being pushed back across the Pacific Ocean by the armed forces of the United States of America. Many officers of the INA were captured and brought to India. Some of them were tried for treason. Then the sad rumour was heard, that Subhas Chandra Bose had died in an aircrash. The treason trials failed in the face of the entire nation's opposition Bose or Netaji, as he was affectionatly called, and his INA, live on in the hearts of millions of Indians.

After the war, once again, elections were held and the Congress formed ministries in all provinces where it had held office earlier and the Muslim league established a stronghold among the Muslims all over India.

All efforts to keep India united were proving unsuccessful. The mischievous British policy of 'Divide and Rule' had borne fruit. The situation was beyond anyone's control. The differences between Hindus and Muslims could no longer be resolved. Hindu-Muslim riots took place in many areas. The British finally decided to leave but the country was to be divided into two separate countries before they did. Gandhiji, Nehru and other Congress leaders reluctantly accepted the idea of partition.

At midnight on 14, August, 1947 the elected leaders of the people gathered in the Central Hall of Parliament. At the stroke of midnight India awoke to new life and freedom. The leaders pledged themselves to the service of the nation and its people. Early on the morning of 15 August, 1947, Jawaharlal Nehru, India's first prime minister, hoisted the Indian tricolour on the Red Fort. India became free and a new age began in the history of our country.

While the entire nation 'broke out' into Independence celebrations, the one man most responsible for it, Gandhiji, was away in Calcutta comforting the victims of the communal riots. Freedom had come tainted with blood. 15 August was like any other day in the life of the Mahatma. He had vowed to devote himself to bring friendship between the Hindus and the Muslims in India. However, within a few months, on 30 January 1948 Gandhiji was shot dead while he was on his way to attend evening prayers at the **Birla House** in Delhi. On his death Jawaharlal Nehru said, 'The light has gone out of our lives, and best prayer we can offer is to give ourselves to truth and carry on the noble work for which he lived and for which he died. He lives in the hearts of millions and will live for immemorial ages'.

Transfer of Power
Midnight 14 August , 1947

Early Troubles

Sardar Vallabhbhai Patel

Independence did not mean all joy and celebration. The country was divided. Pakistan had been formed and the celebrations were mixed with sadness. There were violent communal riots before, during and after Independence.

Gandhiji taught truth, non-violene and communal harmony. But he died a victim of communal bitterness. For some people he appeared to be standing up for Muslims who had caused the partition. The sacred valley of the Indus where the Vedas were first recited had become West Pakistan. A part of Rabindranath Tagore's *Sonar Bangla* (Golden Bengal) had become East Pakistan.

Another cause for sadness was the Kashmir trouble of 1948. **Maharaja Hari Singh** was hesitating about which way to lead his state. Should he join India? Should he stay independent? Raiders from Pakistan helped him to make up his mind.

They invaded Kashmir. The Maharaja speedily agreed to join India. The Indian army was rushed in when all Kashmir was nearly conquered. Indian soldiers showed great dash, bravery and resourcefulness. Most of Kashmir was soon freed from the raiders. The people of Kashmir led by **Sheikh Abdullah,** agreed with the accession signed by their Hindu ruler.

There were still about 600 big and small states ruled by Rajas and Maharajas who were earlier under the protection of the British. Most of these rulers lived in great luxury in large palaces. In free India, where everyone was to be equal, there was no place for independent states or rulers. The task of taking over these states and merging them with the rest of the country was accomplished by Sardar Vallabhbhai Patel, a devoted follower of Gandhiji.

The leaders got down to prepare a new Constitution for Independent India. The Constitution lists the rights of every Indian, and provides guidelines to help the government run the country. The new Constitution came into force on 26 January 1950 and India became a Sovereign Democratic Republic. **Dr. Rajendra Prasad** became the first president and Jawaharlal Nehru the first prime minister of the Republic of India.

Independent India also chose its national symbols. A replica of the Lion Capital of the Ashoka Pillar in which four lions are sitting with their backs to one another, became the state emblem. The pillar had been erected by Emperor Ashoka at Sarnath at the place where Buddha had delivered his first sermon to his disciples. In the centre is a wheel. Below it in the Devnagari script is the inscription *Satyameva Jayate* which means *truth alone prevails.*

The tricolour which kept up the spirit of the people throughout the long struggle for freedom was adopted as the national flag. Its design was slightly changed. The

The State Emblem

charkha was replaced by *chakra* or the Ashoka wheel. The chakra with its 24 spokes, in deep blue is in the centre of a white band. Above it is a band of deep saffron and below it is a band of deep green.

Jana-gana-mana, the song written by Rabindranath Tagore, became the national anthem. The song was first sung on 27 December 1911, at a session of the Indian National Congress.

India is now a **Parliamentary Democracy.** It means that people elect their representatives who meet in what is called the **Parliament** and make laws for the country. No more the kings, emperors or foreign rulers. We rule ourselves through the leaders we elect. Everyone above the

The Tricolour

age of 18 has the right to vote and has a say in electing members of the Parliament and the government. General elections are held every five years. No other country in the world has so many people electing their leaders through free franchise. That is why India is called the largest democracy in the world.

The president is the supreme head of the nation. He is elected by the Parliament for a period of five years. He acts on the advice of a council of ministers which is called the Central Cabinet. The Cabinet is headed by the prime minister. The real powers are with the Central Cabinet. The Central Cabinet is collectively responsible to the Parliament. While the Parliament is responsible for making the laws, the Cabinet headed by the prime minister sees that the laws are implemented.

The country is divide into 25 states and 7 union territories. Each state has a government almost like the one at the centre with a governor, a State Cabinet headed by a chief minister and a State Assembly which is like a small Parliament.

India is now free from foreign rule. It had also wanted to be free from poverty and want, so that its people could live better and contribute their share to the growth of the country. This was not easy to achieve because years of exploitation and neglect had made India a poor country. It was important, therefore, not only to see that more things were produced in the country, but also to see that people had money to buy these things. In other words, it was necessary to plan in order to pull India out of the misery of poverty and make it a strong and self-reliant nation.

For this a group of intelligent people sat together and studied what India's needs were and how they could be met. A **Planning Commission** was set up and it drew up a plan for five years. This was the first **Five Year Plan**. Ever since we have had a new plan after every five years. These plans have ensured our progress towards self-reliance.

Circles of Friendship

Jawaharlal Nehru

When the British ruled, they had defensive rings around their Indian possession.

Jawaharlal Nehru and the other Indian leaders saw no need for defensive rings around India. They chose the way of friendship with all nations.

Shortly after Independence, Pandit Nehru took the lead in the drive to end colonial empires in Asia and Africa. The British gradually gave up all their Asian and African possessions. The Dutch were forced to free Java and the other large islands in the East Indies. Indonesia was formed in this way. The French also left Indo-China. The Portuguese were the last to go.

In this manner, India had a wide circle of friends. There was a circle of friends in the Asian countries

Nehru with Nasser and Tito

which had become free. There was a circle of similar friends in Africa. This was true of Middle East also. Arabs and Indians were friends. For ten years Indians and Chinese described themselves as brothers rather than as friends.

India has been a very active member of the **United Nations**. She did all she could to help the UN to keep peace in the world and to put an end to the making of destructive weapons. At one stage the world was being torn between two very powerful groups of nations. The United States of America and her allies was one group. The Soviet Union (USSR) and her allies was the other group. They made many nuclear bombs. Of course, they fought no terrible wars but they tried to steal a march over each other all the time. There was what is known as a **Cold War** between them. India announced that she was a friend of both groups.

The Cold War continued in Europe. But across the world, in Southeast Asia, a wave of friendship began. Pandit Nehru of India, **Chou En-lai** of China and **Sukarno** of Indonesia put forward the idea of peaceful co-existence. This happened at the **Bandung Conference** in Indonesia in 1955. The five principles for peace that were adopted were called the *Panch Sheel.*

Pandit Nehru went even further. His efforts to ensure peace took him outside Southeast Asia. Nehru, **Nasser** of Egypt and **Tito** of Yugoslavia started the **Non-Aligned Movement.** This was a great big declaration of friendship. The countries which joined the non-Aligned group were, of course, friends among themselves. They also tried to be the friends of the American group and of the Russian group. They even tried to bring these two powerful groups together.

There was another circle of friendship which India entered. This happened about the time the Republic of India was formed. For the benefit of all the old British colonial countries a new arrangement was worked out.

The **Commonwealth Organization** was set up in 1949. The British Crown - the King, or Queen who later succeeded to the throne - was accepted as a symbol of the Commonwealth. India, and most of the other countries in the Commonwealth, accepted the British Crown as a symbolic head only. Pandit Nehru foresaw the benefits India could get from the Organization. He also explained that India had entered it freely and could leave the Commonwealth at any time.

In 1985, India agreed to join the **South Asian Association for Regional Cooperation** (SAARC). President Zia-ur-Rehman of Bangladesh had suggested such an organization.

India, Pakistan, Bangladesh, Sri Lanka, Nepal, Bhutan and the Maldives are members. They look forward to cooperation and friendship. There are many common problems these countries face and if we work together, they can be solved. India is also seeking membership of the **Association of South East Asian Nations** (ASEAN).

India is always keen to join groups which want friendship and are not interested in war. In the next chapter, we will read how India, a peace-loving country, was forced to fight wars.

India has a very important place in the world and an important role to play. India has been hard to work to make the United Nations successful, to stop war and to stop the making of nuclear bombs. India and China together have one third of the people living on our planet, Earth. Every sixth human being is an Indian.

In the disarmament field, India has not signed the **Comprehensive Test Ban Treaty** (CTBT). Why should a few countries which have nuclear weapons keep them and try to stop other countries from getting such weapons? India which has proved its nuclear capability with successful tests in 1974 and again in May 1998,

insists that all countries agree on a time-table for complete removal of nuclear weapons from the face of the earth. If all nuclear weapons are destroyed, then India, will gladly sign such a treaty.

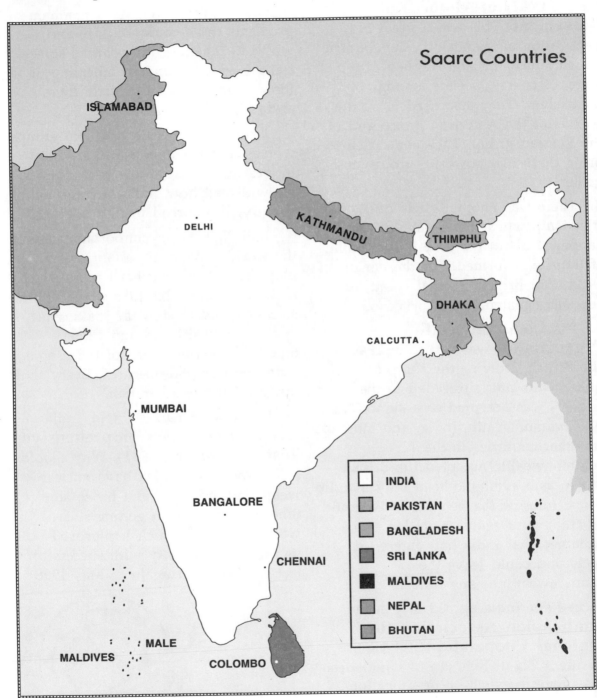

The Wars India Had to Fight

War with China

The Indian Army and the Indian Air Force first saw action in Kashmir. In an earlier chapter it was said that in 1948 raiders from Pakistan invaded Kashmir. They swept through this princely state, plundering the countryside. Maharaja Hari Singh acceded to India and the Indian Army moved into Kashmir. Tanks, artillery and infantry were landed on a frozen lake.

There was no rail link and the road into Kashmir was dangerous. All supplies and reinforcements were flown in by the Air Force. They flew thousands of sorties for aerial survey, for supply and to support Indian soldiers. The weather was bad and, in the whole world, there was no flying space worse than over the Kashmir fighting area. On the ground it was difficult snow-covered terrain. But from the frozen lake where they started their campaign, the Indian Army carried all before them.

At the request of the United Nations, the Indian Army was withdrawn when only a part of Kashmir was left to be freed from the raiders. That part forms what is today called **Pakistan-Occupied Kashmir** (POK). An unofficial boundary line across this area is called the **Line of Actual Control** (LOC).

An uneasy truce is now in force. But the Indian Army could have settled the Kashmir problem there

Indian Soldiers Atop a Captured Tank

and then if they had not been stopped. They could have cleared the whole of Kashmir of the raiders in just a few days. In this first campaign after Independence, there was much heroism and bravery. In this area lies the **Siachen Glacier**, the highest battlefield in the world. Here, Indian and Pakistani troops still face each other in the harshest weather conditions.

In 1962, after flaunting for years the slogan 'Hindi-Chini Bhai-Bhai' the Chinese suddenly made an attack on the Northeastern border of India. Since 1955, the Chinese government had repeatedly agreed with India's stand on Kashmir. But in 1958, popular Indian support–not official–

had gone to the people of Tibet, whom the Chinese had began to suppress.

The **Dalai Lama**, the ruler and the supreme religious leader of the Tibetans, fled with his many followers to India. He was granted political asylum in India. The *Bhai-Bhai* choruses stopped. The Chinese were angry.

An old problem was the India-China boundary line. The Chinese wanted a boundary, hundreds of kilometres to the south, deep in Assam. They pointed out that Tibetans, Bhutanese, Sikkimese, Nagas, Garos, Mizos and Ahoms were racially like the Chinese.

In September 1962 they launched

Lal Bahadur Shastri

heir attack on India's northern
order. India had not opposed
China's policy in Tibet. India, in fact,
ad supported China's claim to her
ightful place in the United Nations.
t never expected a really warlike
ction from the Chinese.

This area was very hard to reach,
nd the forward lines of soldiers had
ot been freshly supplied with
veapons, stores or reinforcements.
ome of the finest fighting men in the
vorld fought a brave war. Nearly a

whole brigade of them gave their
lives as the Army retreated to the
plains of Assam. Here, at last,
supplies and reinforcements reached
them, and gradually our soldiers had
found a better position.

At this stage, the Chinese without
any request from India began, what
they called, a 'unilateral withdrawal'
of their troops. They kept control of
some areas along India's border.
Through friendly discussions, in
recent years, we are still trying to
solve the border problem.

Severe American disapproval,
with secret threats of nuclear attack
by **President Kennedy**, was the
most readily assigned reason for the
Chinese 'unilateral withdrawal'.

About this time, a new dispute
arose between India and Pakistan.
This was over the sharing of the
Indus river waters. India agreed to
pay for the installation of a canal
distribution system. Later, India
found that they were indirectly
paying for the canal system to be
turned into an anti-tank fortification
line. So India protested against this
measure.

Disputes also developed in the
Kutch-Sind area. Pakistan's
aggression in the marshes of the
Rann of Kutch in 1965, was
answered by tank thrusts by the
Indian Army in the Punjab area. The
fighting did not last long. The British
prime minister, **Harold Wilson,**

Surrender at Dhaka

was the peacemaker and the fighting stopped.

Peace talks between the then Indian prime minister, **Lal Bahadur Shastri,** and the Pakistani president, **Ayub Khan,** were held in Tashkent in January 1966. India came out of the war stronger than before. Everyone was confident of the strength of the Indian Armed Forces. The Indian Navy had the upper hand in the Arabian Sea area neighbouring the Kutch sector.

In March 1971, the Pakistan Government set out to crush the **East Pakistan Liberation Movement.** As a result more than ten million Bengali refugees streamed across the border into India. There were many incidents involving Indian border outposts. **Indira Gandhi,** was then the prime minister of India. She repeatedly warned Pakistan. She told the Western nations that India was being pushed into a dangerous situation.

Pakistan commenced full-scale war in the eastern sector in December, 1971. The Indian Army responded by sending in tanks and infantry. A series of brilliant tank battles led to the defeat of Pakistan. A hundred thousand-strong Pakistani army surrendered. **Bangladesh,** a new nation, was formed in place of East Pakistan.

In 1987, India wanted to see a just peace in Sri Lanka. The Sri Lankan government and the militant LTTE (Liberation Tigers of Tamil Elam) had been fighting for some time.

The Sri Lankan president, Jayawardene, asked India's prime minister, **Rajiv Gandhi,** to mediate and send Indian troops to work out a peace settlement on the island.

In a very efficient, combined action, Indian troops were landed. The Indian Air Force and Navy patrolled the Palk Strait and kept watch on Trincomalee harbour to prevent any other country from interfering.

Indians, and particularly the people of Tamil Nadu, were sympathetic to the hard-fighting LTTE. In working out a settlement the LTTE and the Indian Army should have been close friends. But, unfortunately, the LTTE turned against the Indian troops. Neither the Sinhalese nor the Tamils wanted Indian troops to remain in Sri Lanka, despite the wonderful job done by them. In 1989 they were withdrawn from the island. There had been no conflict with the Sri Lankan forces, but the LTTE had to be kept under control and, in controlling them, the Indian Army suffered some loss of life.

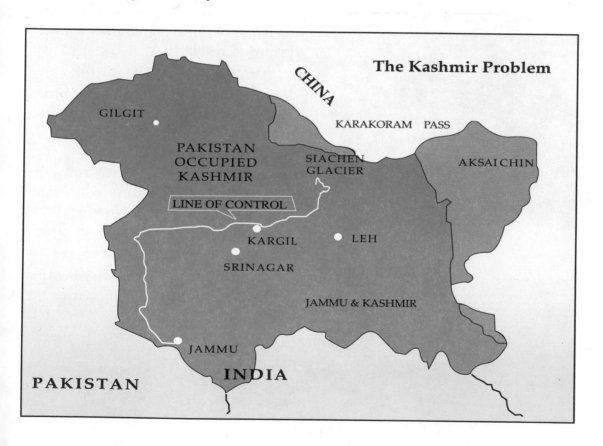

The Best is Yet to Come

Inside India, many things have changed in 50 years. The Indian National Congress (INC) led the people of India to Independence in 1947. Till 1967 there was always a Congress government in New Delhi for the whole country. At the same time, there were Congress governments in almost all the different States of India. Jawaharlal Nehru, Sardar Patel and other giants were in the central government. Each state had its own stalwarts from the days before Independence. **Bidhan Chandra Roy, Profulla Sen and Ajoy Mukherjee** in West bengal, Rajagopalachari in Madras, **Morarji Desai** in Bombay, Govind Ballabh Pant in Uttar Pradesh, **Dr. K.N. Katju in Madhya Pradesh, Sri Krishna Sinha, Dr. Ram Manohar Lohia, Jaiprakash Narain**, in Bihar, **H.K. Mahatab** in Orissa and **Bordoloi** in Assam. These able men were all in the Congress. Jawaharlal Nehru after being the prime minister for 17 years, died in 1964. Lal Bahadur Shashtri became the country's next prime minister.

Different regions had different interest which gradually gave birth and prominence to regional parties. They also had their leaders and parliamentary experts. In pre-Independence days, ability and talent flowed into the Congress which led the fight for freedom. Now equal talent and ability flowered in other parties.

Indira Gandhi, who first became the prime minister in 1966, after the

Indira Gandhi

186

Rajiv Gandhi

udden death of Lal Bahadur Shastri, was undoubtedly a giant in stature. he made the whole world respect ndia. She was respected, loved and eared within the country. She mposed an Emergency in 1975 to emain in power. But in 1977, she greed that there should be fresh eneral Elections. The Congress was efeated. A new government made of lmost all the opposition parties, nited against her, took over in 1977. he Janata Party – *Janata* means the eople, lasted for only three years

under Morarji Desai. For a few months **Charan Singh**, a veteran politician from Uttar Pradesh, became the prime minister.

At this time, Indira Gandhi, out of power, earned back the people's faith in her. In 1980 a fresh election saw her victorious. She was as popular as before. Her second spell as prime minister was quieter than the earlier one. But a major problem was militancy in a section of the great warrior community, the Sikhs. It was led by Bhindranwale, whose followers

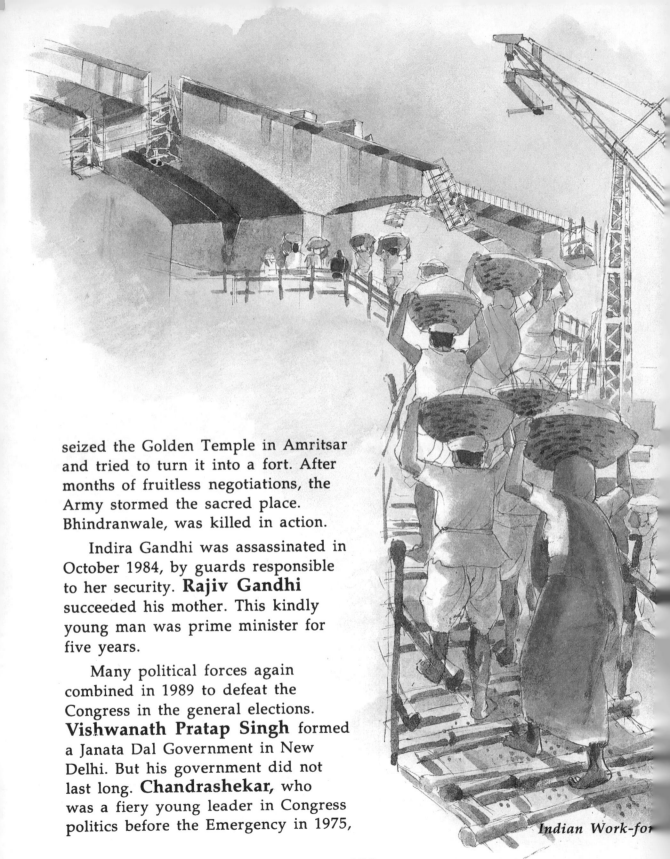

seized the Golden Temple in Amritsar and tried to turn it into a fort. After months of fruitless negotiations, the Army stormed the sacred place. Bhindranwale, was killed in action.

Indira Gandhi was assassinated in October 1984, by guards responsible to her security. **Rajiv Gandhi** succeeded his mother. This kindly young man was prime minister for five years.

Many political forces again combined in 1989 to defeat the Congress in the general elections. **Vishwanath Pratap Singh** formed a Janata Dal Government in New Delhi. But his government did not last long. **Chandrashekar,** who was a fiery young leader in Congress politics before the Emergency in 1975,

Indian Work-for

Indian Industry

became the new prime minister for a few months. Then in 1991, fresh elections became necessary.

After half the elections were over, Rajiv Gandhi made an election tour of Tamil Nadu At **Sriperambudur,** he was assassinated by a young LTTE woman who was a suicide bomber. His death became one of the most tragic casualties of the Sri Lankan Civil War. The Indian people showed their feeling for the Congress and the Gandhi family. Many people voted for the Congress in the second part of the election. **P.V. Narasimha Rao** of the Congress became the new prime minister in 1991.

Over the years other national parties like **Bharatiya Janata Party** and **Lok Dal** have gained in stature and have made their presence felt. They are ably led by experienced leaders such as **Atal Behari Vajpayee, Lal Krishna Advani,**

Indian Railways

Manohar Joshi (BJP) and Vishwanath Pratap Singh (JD). In the states **Jyoti Basu** (Left Front) in West Bengal, **Laloo Prasad Yadav** (Janata Dal) in Bihar, **Jayalalitha** (AIADMK) **Karunanidhi** (DMK) in Tamil Nadu and **N.T. Ramarao** in Andhra have proved popular. In the meantime India's electorate has grown mature and knows the power of the ballot. No party or leader, whether at the centre or in the states, can now take it for granted. Not surprisingly the general elections held in 1995 and 1998 brought to power coalition governments with cruicial roles played by regional parties. These were headed first by **H.D. Deve Gowda, I.K. Gujral (JD)** and later by **A.B. Vajpayee (BJP).**

When we won our freedom in 1947 India as a nation had a great dream. It was a dream to make this country self-reliant; it was a dream to provide food, clothing and shelter to our oppressed teeming millions; a dream to wipe the tears from every eye, as Gandhiji had put it.

On 15 August 1997 India celebrated the golden jubilee or fifty years of Independence. On this occasion people asked, 'Have we achieved all that we set out to achieve?'

Some people felt that the great dream of India lies shattered and we have nothing to be proud about. Many happy people said that Independent India has surpassed the aspirations of its founders and we have a lot to celebrate.

In spite of a succession of external aggressions and internal disturbances we have been able to hold together as one nation. In a country of India's size with so many diverse faiths, languages and cultures, this in itself is a tremendous achievement, if we compare it with the experience of other nations that became independent during this period. We have shown to the world that poverty, illiteracy and a population of bewildering diversity are not obstacles to the growth of a vibrant democracy with all freedoms, especially the freedom of thought and expression, not only guaranteed but exercised.

For the first time the real transfer of power is taking place. It is passing into the hands of people who had been deprived of it for centuries. In H.D. Deve Gowda we had a prime minister who was just an ordinary farmer and in **K.R. Narayanan** we have a president who belongs to the backward classes.

From being a country which did not possess the technique to make pins and needles, India has risen to be the seventh largest industrial nation in the world producing its own automobiles, locomotives, ships, aircraft, missiles, power plants, nuclear fuels, super computers, satellites and satellite launching

The Satellite Launch

Computers

vehicles. It boasts of the largest scientific and technological manpower in the world.

Gone are the days of devastating famines when India had to literally live from 'ship to mouth'. The green revolution has ensured that India is not only self-sufficient but can also export food.

There have been failures too. The galloping rate of population swallows up whatever we produce from our fields and factories. Poverty, illiteracy and unemployment have not been fully tackled. We have yet to provide safe drinking water, shelter, basic health facilities, electricity and other bare necessities of life to a large section of the people. Corruption is corroding the very vitals of our nation. People still fight on the basis of region, religion and caste. Leaders are voted to power not for their ability but because of their religion and caste.

India has great brains, huge resources, a powerful army, great moral values and every sixth person on this earth is an Indian!

We can overcome any problem. What is needed is the collective will of a hitherto easy-going, hesitant and complacement people to lift themselves up economically and socially. We have the capacity to do it and the world at large has taken notice of the fact that India is about to burst on the world scene as a great power.